Hey, Mr. McRay

Answering Teens on Issues of Judgment and Character

Dr. Michael R. McGough

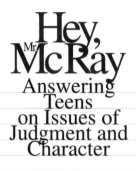

Hey, Mr. McRay

Answering Teens on Issues of Judgment and Character

Dr. Michael R. McGough

Produced and published by
CHARACTER DEVELOPMENT PUBLISHING
for Dr. Michael R. McGough

Edited by Ginny Turner
Cover design by Paul Turley

ISBN 1-892056-14-3
$14.95

*This book is dedicated to
the memory of my father,
Raphael F. McGough
1927-1992*

Table of Contents

Introduction

Personal growth, especially the development of the human character, is a fascinating process that is unique to each individual. However, there are a number of topics, concerns, and issues that most teens will face as they move through the various stages of their adolescent years. For most people, the teen years are filled with more changes in a shorter period of time than any other stage of life. Changes are quick, dramatic, and often unpredictable. During these years, the great human metamorphosis, the transition from child to adult, takes place.

At a time when they most may need advice, teens are often reluctant to ask for help because they are trying to establish a sense of independence. At the same time, their desire to be like everyone else wages a constant battle with their efforts to express their individuality. And as they seek to obtain some adult rights and privileges, they are often quite unaware of the accompanying responsibilities. There is nothing else like the tumultuous teen years.

Hey, Mr. McRay... is a series of letters and responses that appeared in several newspapers as a column under the title "Hey, Mr. McRay: Questions and Answers for Teens." The column first appeared in the *Hanover Evening Sun* (Pennsylvania) in 1990 and was picked up by several other regional papers during the next four years. The weekly columns covered a broad range of adolescent topics. Each column focused on a question or issue relevant to most teens as they develop the character traits they will carry throughout life. Mr. McRay did not offer lofty advice, but instead offered readers a weekly opportunity to consider a specific teen issue. The readers were always given something to think about, and there were usually some words of encouragement and support.

Dr. Michael R. McGough, the educator/writer who is "Mr. McRay," developed the idea for his unique column while watching his own children and his students identify, confront, and work through the various issues that teens encounter. He was recognized for his work with the Frank Manchester Award for Journalistic Excellence given by the Pennsylvania Association of Elementary and Secondary School Principals in 1993.

Suggestions for Using This Book

This book is not intended to be read from front to back or in any specific order. Readers may dip into it here or there—anyplace where a topic catches the eye. Although many of the columns are related, each originally appeared as an independent weekly newspaper column. Scanning the chapter titles and the columns in each chapter will assist readers in finding specific topics among the broad range of issues in the book.

For teens, this book provides an opportunity to explore a variety of issues in which they are currently involved or which they may soon confront. They may feel relieved to realize they are not alone in their feelings on a certain issue. The format of this book provides quick reference to specific topics so readers can select topics most relevant to their own experiences and situations. The advice contained in the columns provides teen readers with something to think about as they seek to address the various issues in their lives.

For parents, *Hey, Mr. McRay...* affords an overview of the years between childhood and adult life. As parents seek to help their teens deal with the numerous situations they will face, this book will provide reminders of what adolescence is like so parents can more easily discern what's on their children's minds. Adults conveniently forget the hopes and disappointments, the frustrations, and the need to fit in that young teens feel. Mr. McRay provides timeless reminders that will undoubtedly stimulate both pleasant and unpleasant memories. Such reminders are a good starting point for helping their children deal with similar experiences. There are times, however, when personal advice from Mom or Dad is rejected just because it is Mom's or Dad's. Suggestions from this book will serve as a source of experience and information that is not the child's or the parent's, and may be a starting point for meaningful discussions in the home.

For teachers and school counselors, *Hey, Mr McRay...* is an educational resource that can be used as a part of a number of learning opportunities. Specific topics can be assigned, or students can be given the opportunity to select topics of specific interest to them. The letters at the beginning of each column can be used as writing prompts with the students providing the answers. The response provided by Mr. McRay can then be compared and contrasted with those developed by the students. Students facing any number of situations in their lives often choose not to talk about them. This book gives teachers and counselors another resource to share with students who may be reluctant to discuss their concerns one-on-one. The perspective offered by Mr. McRay may make discussion easier and more frequent.

For anyone interested in teens, the issues they face, and the ways in which they address the concerns in their lives, *Hey, Mr. McRay...* is a valuable resource. Helping our teens develop the essential and appropriate character traits to guide them into and throughout their adult lives is a major challenge to us all that demands shared commitment. And as has always been true, our future is only as good as the prudent investments we make in the youth of today!

PEERS

Helping a Friend Feel Secure
Dealing with Abusive Behavior
When Smoking Is a Problem
Making New Friends
Friendships Change As You Do
Teasing about Faith Not Uncommon
Preserving a Friendship
A Friendship with Strings Attached
Drivers Must Be Licensed
Racial Issues Cloud a Friendship
Words Have the Power to Hurt
Getting Attention Is Not Always Good
Student's Racism Reflects Badly on His Friends
Several Good Lessons to Be Learned
Drug Use Shows Recklessness

Hey, Mr. McRay,

One of my best friends gets down on herself all the time. She starts out everything she does by saying she can't do it, or she's not going to do it right. If she's just doing everyday things, she's fine. It's when she has to do something special that she really gets herself all tied up in knots. Since we're good friends, I always try to be there for her, but sometimes it's hard. I get nervous, too, but I have to take care of her. Like when we tried out for cheerleading. I was so worried about her I didn't concentrate on what I was doing. Neither of us made the squad, and that is OK, but I know I didn't do my best.

She's been like this for a long time. Some of our other friends say she's just acting like that to get attention, and they don't have time for that. My mother understands that I want to be a good friend, but she says I shouldn't let another person's insecurities drag me down too. I don't know what to do. Do you have any suggestions?

Sincerely,
Gina

Helping a Friend Feel Secure

Dear Gina,

I do have some suggestions you might wish to consider. But first, I want you to know your mother's advice is right where I will begin: You can accomplish nothing by making yourself the victim of another person's problem.

Although it's often difficult to admit to others, most of us have some fears that we deal with, either daily or just occasionally. Maybe you have a fear of heights, a fear of speaking in front of a room full of people, or a fear that you'll develop some serious health problem. For most people, such fears are not a daily problem. When problem situations do arise, most people have developed strategies for dealing with fear and getting beyond it. A more formal term for these strategies is "coping mechanisms." These coping mechanisms allow us to face fears and uncertainties and deal with them. Even though we may not "win," most of us can at least deal with problem situations.

Your friend has made you her coping mechanism. You are what permits her to deal with her fears. As you discovered during your cheerleading tryouts, assuming such a role, even for a good friend, can place a significant burden on you. Such a burden can have a very negative effect on your ability to deal with situations. In the end, no one really gains. Instead, you both are forced to function under the shadow of her fears and self-doubts.

Since you have been a source of support for your friend for some time, I don't suggest you abruptly drop her. Instead, start helping her to deal with her fears. Begin to send the message that it will not help her to get over her fears and doubts if she always shares them with you. Your friend must come to realize that if she is ever going to conquer her doubts and fear of failure, she must do it herself. Neither you nor anyone else can do it for her!

The idea that she may simply be trying to get attention is possible, but if this has been going on for some time, I doubt it. I think your friend has never developed strategies for dealing with her daily fears. As you try to help her assume ownership of her fears and anxieties, share some strategies you have found to be successful. As you do this, you'll be fulfilling the obligations you feel you owe your friend, and at the same time you'll be helping her to take control of her own life.

Hey, Mr. McRay,

I know this person who verbally molests people in sexual ways. People he's talked to this way are my friends, and I'm scared he might start talking to me that way. I can't avoid him because I see him every day. What should I do?

—Scared and Confused

Dealing with Abusive Behavior

Dear Scared and Confused,

It would be nice if I could tell you that such situations are rare, but they are not. There are many people who abuse or "molest" others with words. In the situation you describe, the person abuses people with inappropriate sexual comments. Others abuse people with insults, degrading comments, false rumors, praise that has no meaning, or promises they have no intention of keeping. These various forms of verbal abuse all have one thing in common: They hurt the people to whom they are directed. Whether the person making the comments is trying to hurt others or not, verbal abuse is inappropriate, and no one has the right to willfully hurt or abuse others.

Language is meant to communicate. Words can be used to communicate knowledge, to share feelings, to inquire and seek information, or to share thoughts, both great and small. However, language can also be used to spread hatred, to promote mistrust, to create discomfort, and to generally make others feel "scared and confused." The use of language is determined by the speaker. The listener decides if the words are worth accepting. Understanding this, there are several ways you might deal with the person you describe.

If ignored long enough, most people catch the hint that they have no audience. If this person finds himself without an audience, he will either have to clean up his act or learn to enjoy talking to himself. If you attempt this, do not expect immediate results. It may take time, and you might have to say something like, "Hey, no one appreciates your crude comments, so keep it clean or keep it to yourself!"

If ignoring him and some simple, direct comments don't make the point, consider seeking help. Inappropriate comments of a sexual nature are not only unpleasant, but are a violation of your rights. There are laws to protect individuals from abusive or harassing comments from others. You might have to involve your parents, a teacher, a counselor, or one of the principals at your school. Explain your situation carefully and completely. Be prepared to give specific examples. Don't avoid seeking help because you are afraid he will retaliate. If you do, you are allowing him to control you with your own fear. A school should be a place where students feel safe and free to learn, experience, and grow. If you are constantly "scared and confused" and trying to avoid a particular person, it will be difficult for you to accomplish much else.

Hey, Mr. McRay,

I drive to school almost every day. Some of my friends ride with me. One of the girls who rides with us sometimes smokes. We have all dropped some hints that we don't like it when she smokes, but we haven't just come out and told her. We're afraid we'll hurt her feelings. It makes our clothes and our hair stink, and who wants to start school like that? She doesn't ride with us every day, but when she does, her smoking is a real pain. We like her, but we don't like her cigarettes. Maybe we are making too much of this, but we don't know how to tell her. If smoking bothered you, how would you let someone know without hurting them or making them mad?

—Yours,

Dillon

When Smoking Is a Problem

Dear Dillon,

I have never smoked, and like you and your friends, I do not like the smell of smoke on my clothes. I also do not like to breathe smoke, particularly when I am in a confined area like a car or a small room.

You are perfectly within your rights to tell her that you do not want her to smoke in your car anymore. I can understand and appreciate your desire not to hurt her feelings or embarrass her. However, if handled properly you can get your message across.

Some time ago, I had to face a situation similar to the one you describe. I cannot say the way I handled it was right, or that it will work for you, but it worked for me. I waited for an opportunity to speak to the person privately and explained that her smoking was causing some problems and concerns for those exposed to her secondhand smoke. I emphasized that our problem had nothing to do with her as a person, but we were annoyed by her smoking. In that way, I was able to clearly make smoking, not the person, the problem.

Years of research and experience indicate that there is a very strong link between smoking and the health risks faced by the smoker. As the research continues, there is a growing amount of evidence to indicate that secondhand smoke is also closely linked to a number of health problems. (Secondhand smoke is the smoke inhaled by anyone other than the smoker.) In addition to the potential health problems, the unpleasant odors of cigarettes left behind on clothes, hair, and furniture are also a problem for the nonsmoker.

Since the early 1970s, there has been a growing trend away from cigarette smoking. Today only about a third of the population of the United States smokes. Nonsmokers are clearly in the majority, and they are no longer a silent majority. Demands for clean air and the rights of nonsmokers have prompted the adoption of "No Smoking" policies in most public buildings, and where smoking is permitted, nonsmoking areas are usually provided.

Beyond the fact that the girl who smokes is a guest in your car and should not smoke without your permission, she has no right to expose you and your friends to the dangers of secondhand smoke. She also has no right to fill your car with unpleasant odors that cling to your hair and clothes. If you decide to tell your friend, make smoking in your car the point of your concern, not her.

Hey, Mr. McRay,

Making new friends has never been easy for me. I'm quiet around other people. I'm in middle school this year, and there are many students I didn't go to elementary school with. I've been trying to make some new friends, but no one seems to pay any attention to me. There's no problem when I first meet people, but soon they just lose interest in me. I'm very careful not to say anything to hurt someone's feelings, and I always listen when someone is talking to me. I try never to talk about myself because most people don't like it when someone is always talking about herself. I wish I knew what I was doing wrong because I want to make some new friends.

—Yours,

Theresa

Making New Friends

Dear Theresa,

Take a minute to think about some of the new kids at your school with whom you'd like to become friends. What do you know about them, their families, or where they live? What they like to do in their spare time, or where they "hang out" after school? What they are interested in, or what they may want to do after high school?

My guess is that you know a good deal about the people you'd like to be your friends. It's what we know about people that most often causes us to want to be friends with them. How much have you shared about yourself? Do any of the new students in your school know what you are interested in, where you spend your spare time, or anything about your family? From your letter, I'd guess that they don't. Your elementary classmates know you because you've been together for at least one year. The new students in your classes know very little about you, and you are not sharing.

An important part of being a good friend is being a good listener. However, another part of being a good friend is a willingness to share. It's not necessary to share every detail of your past or to discuss every notion you have about the future, but you must share enough to allow people to get to know you. I agree that people who constantly talk about themselves are not pleasant to be around. But on the other hand, it can be difficult to be friends with someone you know nothing about. You may have a great deal in common with many of the new students in your school, but if you never share, they will never know. You need not talk about yourself all the time to begin sharing a little about yourself. It is not an either/or situation. When you are around some people you would like to get to know, be an active participant in the conversation. This means being both a listener and a speaker. For example, if the conversation is centered on weekend activities, say or mention what you like to do. You will be letting others know that you are interested in what they are talking about, and you will be sharing a little about yourself. There's a balance between talking too much and talking too little. Experiment to find the balance that works best for you.

Hey, Mr. McRay,

Sarah and I started kindergarten together. She's always been my best friend, but lately she doesn't seem to have time for me. She's going with a guy in our class named Brad. They really like each other and are together all the time. When they're not, they're on the phone, or Sarah is waiting for him to call. Sarah and I used to be like sisters. We were always either together or on the phone, and now I'm just taken for granted. She only has time for me when Brad is not around.

I don't want them to think I'm trying to horn in on their friendship, so I don't go around Sarah when she is with Brad. I'll admit I am jealous, but I don't want to come between them. I still want to be Sarah's friend, but I don't know how since she started going with Brad.

—Signed, Renée

Friendships Change As You Do

Dear Renée,

You and your friend Sarah are growing up, and a big part of this process is adapting to change. Your friendship with Sarah is changing, and you must be prepared to adapt to that change.

It sounds like Sarah and Brad have a strong interest in each other. Because of this interest, they focus much of their time and attention on each other. This is normal during the initial stages of most new relationships. New relationships, friendships, or interests often become very consuming. A new job, a membership in a new club, even a new hobby can consume almost all a person's interest. Usually, this initial period of intense interest is followed by a more balanced approach.

Have you discussed your feelings with Sarah? Before you assume she is simply taking your friendship for granted, you owe it to her and yourself to share how you feel. You said you don't want to come between Sarah and Brad, and that is understandable. However, don't stand by and let your friendship with Sarah deteriorate. Old friendships need not be sacrificed when new ones are made. You mentioned that you stay away from Sarah when she's with Brad. You may be doing this because you don't want to appear to be "horning in" on them, but it may seem to Sarah that you have lost interest in your friendship with her. You may be sending her the wrong signal.

Life will involve you in many relationships, some casual and some close and intense. Each of these may go through stages over time, from very active to casual to almost passive. You will enjoy both short relationships and relationships that last a lifetime. My guess is that Sarah values your friendship. Don't make her choose between you and Brad. Let her have the opportunity to be friends with both of you!

Hey, Mr. McRay,

Last week I told some friends at my lunch table what I had done over the weekend. I went on a two-day retreat with the youth group from my church, and I told them how much fun I had and some of the things we did. Ever since, they have been calling me "Saint Matthew." I didn't preach to them or even talk about religion. I just had a good time and I wanted to tell them about it.

My best friend, Ryan, isn't really teasing me that much. I want to invite him to go with me the next time our youth group has an activity, but I know he'll say "No" because he won't want to be teased. I'm not ashamed of going to church or being part of a church youth group, but I don't like being teased, and I don't want that nickname to stick. I can't say anything to my parents because they would probably call the school, and that would only make it worse for me. What would you do?

—Signed, Matt

Teasing about Faith Not Uncommon

Dear Matt,

Throughout most of human history, people have been made fun of, persecuted, ridiculed, and even killed because of their religious beliefs. Even though religious freedom has been guaranteed countless times through constitutions, laws, and court rulings, there will always be those who find it difficult to accept religion as the highly personal matter that it is. Although the teasing you are taking is far from the mental and physical harassment others have faced, it is nonetheless a problem with which you must deal.

One solution is simply to ignore the comments your friends are making. Like most adolescent teasing, it will probably go away on its own, and the nickname will not stick. If this doesn't happen, you might try telling your friends that you do not appreciate their comments, and that if they cannot "back off with the Saint Matthew stuff," you would like to be left alone! Maybe they don't know how uncomfortable they are making you. If you are still unable to make your point, you have two sources of potential help. Discuss the situation with your school guidance counselor. Often counselors are able to explain things in ways that make them easier for people your age to understand. Your counselor may decide to have a private chat with some of your friends.

I can appreciate your concerns about involving your parents. However, you must remember that your parents were once adolescents, and they more than likely remember a little about teasing and nicknames. Do not rule out talking with your parents. Explain the problem you are having. Tell them that if they get too involved it may only make things worse.

It sounds like your friend Ryan understands your situation and has no desire to make it worse for you. It might be a good idea to give him the opportunity to take part in your youth group activities. In fact, inviting Ryan to join you might become part of the solution. Don't assume that all your friends have no interest in church activities. Insensitive friends and their actions are not a good reason to avoid something that has meaning for you.

Hey, Mr. McRay,

One of my best friends and I started taking tennis lessons about a year ago. At first we were equally bad, but I really like tennis, and because I play every chance I get, my game is getting better all the time. My friend doesn't like it that much, and he's not doing very well now. We're not as good friends as we were before we started taking tennis lessons. I don't want to destroy our friendship, but I want to keep playing tennis. I thought about slacking off a little to save our friendship. Do you think this will work?

—Yours, Greg

Preserving a Friendship

Dear Greg,

I can't predict if you will be able to preserve your friendship if you slack off on your tennis game. However, if your friendship is based on a comparison of your tennis abilities, I would say you have a shallow friendship.

Skills, abilities, and interests vary greatly from person to person. That is part of what makes us different and contributes to our individuality. The world would be a boring place if we were all exactly the same. On the other hand, many people share common interests and the talents needed to develop those interests. Friendships are based on a combination of these differences and similarities. Two friends may have a great deal in common, but they will more than likely also have many individual characteristics that are different, maybe even opposite.

One of the major building blocks of a solid and enduring friendship is respect. Respect should involve all aspects of a friendship and must include both common and unique characteristics. Thomas Edison, the inventive wizard, and Henry Ford, America's automotive pioneer, were very close friends. Their genius, their understanding of the technologies of the early 20th century, and their skills in marketing were obvious similarities. But they also had vast differences in their personal lives, the forces that motivated them, and the social causes in which they were interested. During their long friendship, both Edison and Ford lived through numerous failures and successes. However, their friendship continued because they shared a strong common respect for each other.

Hey, Mr. McRay,

One of my friend's parents own a cottage at a lake. They have a boat and there's a swimming pool and a lodge there. She has invited me to go to their cottage for a weekend, and I've been really looking forward to it. That is, until recently. We are friends, but not really best friends or anything. We live in the same neighborhood, and we've been in school together since kindergarten.

Ever since she asked me to go and my parents said I could, she's been different to me. She gets angry if I don't sit with her at lunch, and last weekend I stayed over at another friend's house, and she got really mad. She said she thought I was her best friend and she may take someone else to her cottage. I didn't know what to say to her. I felt bad, but it wasn't like I did anything to hurt her. Do you think it was wrong for me to sleep over at my other friend's house?

—Belinda

A Friendship with Strings Attached

Dear Belinda,

No! You have every right to have many friends, and just because someone has invited you for a weekend trip, she doesn't have the right to control your circle of friends. It sounds as if she's using an invitation as a "bribe" to force you to have her as your best, and maybe only, friend. She has placed you in an unfair position, and I suggest you take some steps to get out of it.

Unfortunately, you will find that when some people offer you something, they expect something in return. This is sometimes referred to as "giving something with strings attached." In your situation, you have been given a weekend at a lake, and in return (this is the string that is attached) you are expected to have only one best friend. To my way of thinking, this is a pretty expensive price to pay for a weekend at a lake.

Before your friend ties any more strings to her weekend offer, I suggest you have a talk with her. Tell her you appreciate her offer and are looking forward to spending a weekend with her and her family. However, also tell her that you have other friends you will not ignore. Try to explain that you are interested in having many friends. If she seems to understand and accept what you are saying, try to involve her with your other friends. Invite her to sit with you and some of your friends at lunch. If you're having a party at your house, invite her. If you are invited to other parties, ask if she also could be invited. In this way, you will be treating her as a friend while maintaining your other friendships. On the other hand, if she doesn't understand or accept your position, you will have to make a decision. Is a weekend at a lake worth having someone else limit and control your circle of friends?

Hey, Mr. McRay,

My boyfriend is 16, but he doesn't have his driver's license yet. His older brother taught him how to drive, and he says he's ready to take his test. My boyfriend's parents want him to wait another month and practice some more. My boyfriend said his brother will let him use his car to take me out before he passes his test. I want to go out with him, but I'm afraid we might get caught. If I tell him I don't want to go out, he might want to break up with me. I am not sure what I should do. Do you have any suggestions?

—Truly, Becki

Drivers Must Be Licensed

Dear Becki,

I have a very direct and specific suggestion for you—do not ride with your boyfriend until he has his license! Regardless of how well your boyfriend may be able to handle a car, driving without a valid operator's license is a violation of the law. There are also penalties for the owner of the car and those who permit unlicensed drivers to operate a motor vehicle.

Driving is a privilege that most citizens enjoy on a daily basis. It is difficult for me to imagine being without a driver's license, and I recall how eager I was to get my license. Today, I am still pleased to have the freedom of movement that driving provides. However, in order to have that freedom, a number of laws must be obeyed. Many years ago, a driver's license was available for only the payment of a small fee. However, because the number of cars has grown, the speed they travel has increased, and the road network has expanded, it was necessary to establish laws to regulate the operating of motor vehicles. One of them was the requirement of having a valid driver's license. This was done for the protection of all.

Let your boyfriend know that you are not interested in riding with him until he has received his driver's license. If he is unable to accept your decision and attempts to pressure you into going with him, I think you need to reconsider your friendship. In addition to being involved in an illegal activity, you will be riding with a driver who has not yet demonstrated that he can operate an automobile safely.

If your boyfriend suggests you're wrong for not going with him, remind him he's showing you very little respect. He is inviting you to take part in something he knows is wrong. What kind of person would ask a friend to do this? Consider this seriously. If you know your boyfriend's brother well enough, you might wish to talk with him. Explain your fears and ask him not to let his brother borrow his car until he can legally drive it. If you are unable to make your boyfriend understand that what he wants to do is both illegal and dangerous, you might need to mention something to your parents or to his parents. Though you may feel you are causing a problem for him by doing so, you may be preventing a bigger and more serious situation from developing.

Hey, Mr. McRay,

I am white and I have a friend who is black. We live close to each other, so we go to the same school. When we were little, we played a lot together, and at home we are friends, but at school she doesn't want to have anything to do with me. Tara will say "Hi," but that's about it. She has her friends at school and so do I. My school friends are all white, and her school friends are all black. This does not seem right to me since we are friends out of school. I asked her to sit with my friends and me at lunch, but she said she couldn't. I asked my friends if she could sit with us, and they said I should just leave her alone.

I asked my mother about this, and she said the problem is not with Tara and me; the problem might be with our friends. She said our friends may be setting expectations for us of how we have to act at school. She said I should talk to Tara and let her know I want to be friends whether we are in school or at home. Do you think this is a good idea?

—Monica

Racial Issues Cloud a Friendship

Dear Monica,

It is most definitely a good idea—being friends is always a good idea. What your mother has shared with you is unfortunately all too true in many instances. This may be a new and troubling situation to you and your friend, but it is by no means a new problem. This dilemma has plagued the human race since the beginning of time.

As you well know, we are not all the same in all aspects. Race, religion, nationality, language, sex, education, financial status, and general personality are just a few of the characteristics that make every person unique. In an ideal world, we all would appreciate and enjoy what makes us unique and different. Unfortunately, this is not always the case. In fact, the characteristics that make us unique have often become the reasons for isolation, bigotry, hatred, and war.

For you and Tara, the difference in your race is not a problem. However, to your friends that difference may be a problem. Their way of dealing with the difference is to isolate themselves. I don't know how much pressure your friends may be putting on you, but they may have raised it to a loyalty issue, thereby forcing you to make a choice as to whose friend you want to be—those in the group who are alike, or Tara, who is different. Such pressure can be tough to handle, but don't give up. You may not be able to change the world, but if you can destroy a little prejudice or bigotry, you have helped to clean up your little corner of the world. Remember that courtesy is appropriate in all situations— smiling at and greeting a friend is never the wrong thing to do.

This may not be a situation that can be resolved easily or quickly, and you may need some help. You should probably start by talking to Tara one-on-one. Do not be confrontational or make accusations. Instead, just share that you want to be friends whether you are in school or at home. Since you and Tara have been friends a long time, my guess is that she will be open with you. It might take some time to work through this, so be patient. Ask your parents for advice, too. They should be able to help you deal with this situation.

Some problems are so thorny they can't be solved in a single generation, but don't see this as a hopeless situation. Hang on to your friendship with Tara, and believe in the power of individuals to find solutions to age-old problems.

Hey, Mr. McRay,

My friends and I are always together in school, and we're together at night and on weekends. We know most everyone in our school, and we're always talking about someone in our class. It seems that's all we do. Some of what we say is true, but sometimes we just make stuff up so we'll have something to say. I'm not saying that I'm better than my friends or anything, but I really think always talking about people is wrong. I don't want to spend so much time talking about everybody. What do you think I should do?

—Yours, Lynn

Words Have the Power to Hurt

Dear Lynn,

You have already taken two big steps. You have identified a problem, and you have decided to do something about it. As you know, you and your friends have developed a bad habit. Fortunately, you are aware of this and you want to make a change. Let's hope your friends will share your concern and will want to follow your example.

People talk about each other for different reasons. We are interested in our peers, and sharing what we know about others is common. Rest assured that you and your friends did not invent gossiping. However, sharing what we know about others becomes a problem when it's intended to hurt or do damage. Words are very powerful. They have the power to tear down and the power to build up. What we say can encourage others or disable them. Making up and spreading rumors about people can seriously undermine a person's reputation. Our words can calm a troubled situation, or they can make it worse. Tragically, not everyone is aware of the potential power of what they say. They have either underestimated the impact of their words, or they don't think they will be taken seriously. They hurt others without ever intending to do so. As you know, there are also plenty of people who willingly set out to hurt others. They know what they are saying and that they are hurting someone or at least making them uncomfortable. Whether we intend to hurt others or not, we are all responsible for what we say.

Hoping that your friends will totally stop talking about other people is a bit unrealistic, but learning to control the quantity and tone of your talk is a realistic goal. If you don't want to discuss this directly with your friends, you might get your message across through your own example. When your friends fall into a "gossiping frenzy," ask yourself these simple questions before you add anything to the conversation:

1. Is what I'm about to say true?
2. Would I say this if the person I'm talking about were standing here?
3. What is the purpose of sharing what I'm about to say?
4. Would I want someone to say this about me?

Though we may not always admit it, most of us do care what others say about us, even if it gets back to us through another person. From time to time we all hear second-hand comments that have been made about us, and we've probably had our private comments about another shared with the person we talked about. When you talk about others behind their backs, you have little control over whether or how your comments will be later repeated. Keeping this in mind, never say anything about someone you wouldn't say in his or her presence.

Hey, Mr. McRay,

I have a tough question for you. It's something my friends and I have talked about, but we can't figure it out. Why are the kids who cause the most trouble in and out of school so popular? Why do they get all the attention, and why are people so interested in them?

One boy in ninth grade has been arrested several times and has been suspended from school more times than you can count. There are always girls who are interested in him, and the guys around school are always talking about him. It's like he's a hero or something. One of my friends now thinks the best way to become popular is to get in trouble. I don't feel that way, but I don't understand. Am I missing something?

—Dan

Getting Attention Is Not Always Good

Dear Dan,

The situation you describe is difficult to explain. The first thing you and your friends need to do is clarify your definition of a "hero." To me, a hero is a person whom you admire and respect, someone you would like to be like. Our heroes are people whose words, thoughts, and actions win our respect and admiration. These can be individuals in history, sports, or public service, or perhaps family members or significant people in our lives, such as a teacher or coach. Even though we might not want to change places with them, they give us personal and professional goals to strive for. Our heroes win our attention in a positive way.

Other people, who are anything but heroes, also attract our attention with their words, thoughts, and actions. But we most definitely do not want to change places with them, and they do not set examples we would like to follow. They may win our attention, but it is negative attention.

I think that you, your friends, and millions of other teenagers frequently confuse negative and positive attention. All you see is that the problem students in your school receive more attention from the teachers and administrators, and they are frequently a topic of conversation among their peers.

Currently, there are several popular television programs that bring both dramatizations and actual videos of crime right into our homes. These criminals may have won our attention, but they are definitely not heroes. When you see a story on the evening news about a murder, a robbery, or a major drug-related arrest, the people involved have won our attention. They are in the spotlight, and many people are interested in hearing about what they have done. However, what they have done is not admirable. Keep these examples in mind when you begin drawing a line of distinction between true popularity and simple negative attention.

Hey, Mr. McRay,

I have a good friend who always makes comments about blacks. He tells racial jokes and knows all kind of funny lines about blacks. He says that he's not a bigot and he's not prejudiced against blacks. He says that he's just joking and doesn't mean any harm. He said he would never do anything to hurt anyone and he would never tell his jokes around blacks. He has a Confederate flag that he puts in the window of his car sometimes. He says that's just a joke too.

Some of the things he says get laughs, and that seems to make him do it even more. I don't think what he is doing is right. Even if we believe him that he doesn't mean any harm, other people who hear him may not understand that. I want him to know I don't like his comments and I'm embarrassed to be with him when he makes them. My problem is that I don't want to confront him and make a big issue of it all. Got any ideas?

—Dave

Student's Racism Reflects Badly on His Friends

Dear Dave,

Whether he says he is joking or not, your friend is wrong. Racial slurs and bigoted comments are not appropriate, regardless of the intentions of the person making them. Your uneasy feelings are understandable. Your desire to do something about your feelings is one upon which you should act. Uncomfortable feelings, regardless of the situation in which you find yourself, are usually a good indication that something is wrong.

Comedians, authors, and the producers of movies and plays have made millions of dollars playing on the stereotypical characteristics of various races and nationalities. By so doing they have reinforced those stereotypical perceptions to the point where there are those who believe or at least accept them to have some degree of truth. This is the point where "harmless humor" turns to bigotry, which is a deep-seated hatred. Bigotry is anything but harmless.

Perceptions are powerful and tend to become reality over a period of time. For example, your friend feels that he is just kidding around with his jokes, comments, and his Confederate flag, but the perceptions of others may be dramatically different. Many people may well see him as a bigot or a racist based on his behavior. You clearly indicate that you do not agree with his words and actions.

At this point, you have two options. You can do nothing, and your friend will probably continue to act as he has been and will assume that you agree with him. Or, you can share your concerns with your friend in the hope that he will change. If he chooses to continue with his racial comments, slurs, and jokes, you have two more options. You can either put up with his words and actions, or you can find other company. If you are uncomfortable or don't like being linked with that kind of behavior and attitude, the choice seems to be clear and simple.

Advice my mother shared with me years ago is still sound today and may serve you well as you consider your options: "You are judged by the company you keep."

Hey, Mr. McRay,

I have this friend I wrote a note to. It had some things about my boyfriend in it. I told her not to show him or anyone else, but she showed him anyway. This got me mad at her. I said a few ignorant words, and now my friend and I aren't talking. What should I do? Should I hold this against her?

—Signed, Melody

Several Good Lessons to Be Learned

Dear Melody,

The situation you describe has a number of good lessons in it.

Lesson 1: Don't write or say things that you don't want repeated. Even when you share your thoughts in confidence, there is always a chance the person you have trusted may break that trust. This won't happen every time you take someone into your confidence, but when you share your thoughts and feelings, you must always consider the possibility that what you are sharing may reach other people.

Lesson 2: "Ignorant" words, whether spoken on purpose or in haste, usually accomplish nothing. A wise man once said, "Only those who have little knowledge of and little respect for the English language use the more unpleasant words it contains." No truer words were ever spoken. Profanity, ignorant words, vulgar slang, and the like are generally offensive and add little to a conversation.

Lesson 3: Until those involved in a disagreement take time to discuss their problems, there is little chance of a solution. Ignoring your friend may give you some comfort or satisfaction. You may even feel as though you are punishing her for betraying your trust. However, you are also punishing yourself. She was your friend, and maybe she will be your friend again. Before you cast her aside, give her an opportunity to explain what she did and why she did it. There's a chance there are details of which you are unaware.

Lesson 4: Grudges are very heavy things, and holding them takes effort and can be a real burden. What has happened between you and your friend is done. The note has been shared, and nothing you can do is going to change that. You are left with one of two options. You can carry a grudge, remain angry, and build a wall between you and your friend. Or, you could talk to your friend, explain the position she put you in, and listen to what she has to say. Talking to her may or may not solve the problem. However, though there is no guarantee that you can talk this problem out, you'll have a far better chance of finding a solution by talking to her than by ignoring her.

Hey, Mr. McRay,

I am writing this letter for a friend. She is into marijuana, and I think she uses it a lot more than she should. I've tried to tell her she can become dependent on marijuana and not be able to quit. She says she is in control and can stop any time she wants. She said that is the good part about marijuana that it is not addictive. I also tried to tell her that marijuana is the type of drug that can lead you into taking stronger drugs that are more addictive. I think talking to her is a waste of time because she has her mind made up that marijuana is no problem. I'll admit I did it with her once, but it scared me and I stopped for good. She thinks I'm weak because I can't use it and control how much I use. If you'll respond to my letter, I'll share it with her.

—Michele

Drug Use Shows Recklessness

Dear Michele:

If your friend or you are using marijuana, or have in the past, you are using it too much. Regardless of all else, it is illegal. Arguments for legalization of marijuana and other drugs have been around for decades, and I suspect they will be around for decades to come. Nevertheless, the current legal statutes are clear—marijuana is a controlled substance.

In no way will I condone your use of marijuana, even if you only used it once. On the other hand, you have made a prudent decision not to use any more, and your concern for your friend is admirable. Her lack of appreciation for your concern is going to frustrate your efforts to influence her thinking. Don't let this stop you from trying. Depending on your friend's age and her current family status, you may want to involve other members of her family or other friends. Maybe several voices offering similar advice will get through to her. For what they may be worth, either share the following thoughts or let her read them for herself. I'm not an expert on drugs. I have no personal experience with the use of drugs, but I'm aware of contemporary drug research, and I'm familiar with the harsh lessons drug users have shared as a result of their experiences.

Drugs can and do affect different people differently. Assuming that you can safely indulge in a certain drug because someone you know is doing so ignores this fact. Few people who use drugs do so because they believe it is a legal, morally correct, or healthy pastime. They do so for many other reasons, all of which are essentially excuses. Are those who ask others to join them in drug use doing so out of the desire to share something good, or are they asking so they can justify their actions on the premise that everyone else is doing it too? I am reminded of the adage "Misery loves company." It's a similar situation with alcohol—no one likes or wants to be a lonely drunk.

Certain drugs, and marijuana is a notable one, are known as **gateway drugs**. In fact, there is a great deal of research that indicates that the nicotine in cigarettes is also a gateway drug. A gateway drug is one that establishes an introduction to the use of other drugs. There is a great deal of research to indicate that most hardcore drug users began their habit of drug use with gateway drugs.

The level of emotional, social, and physical impairment that marijuana causes depends on several variables. However, it is beyond question that marijuana use, even just occasionally, can result in a wide array of impairments. The duration of these impairments is also dependent on many variables. To ignore that there is a distinct and direct relationship between marijuana use and impairments is foolhardy and irresponsible. Unfortunately, many people who use drugs, including alcohol, suffer impairments that impact others besides themselves. Drunk drivers are a perfect example. Do I need to mention the difficulties you'll cause yourself and your family if you get arrested for drug possession? Are you aware that most job applications ask if you've been convicted of a felony?

The choice not to use drugs is not a sign of weakness. On the contrary, making responsible choices is an indication of internal strength and willpower. Dabbling with drugs while assuring yourself you can quit at any time is reckless, indicating a lack of understanding of the potential dangers and consequences of drug involvement. It's serious business.

SCHOOL

Cheerleading Causes Rift among Friends
Coping with a Teacher Who Is Unfair
New Student's Stories Are Hard to Believe
Student's Rage Is a Reason to Intervene
In the Middle of a Dilemma
Concealed Weapon More Danger Than Security
Judgment Needed for E-mail Use
Teen Needs to Get Organized
Volunteering Should Be a Reward in Itself
Senior Boy Asked the Wrong Girl to the Prom
Asking for Help Is a Smart Thing to Do
Should You Report a Cheater?
It's Impossible to Please Everyone
It's Never Too Late to Change Your Reputation
Achievement Doesn't Make Someone a Loser
Labels Don't Do Justice
Should Student Athletes Get Special Privileges?

Hey, Mr. McRay,

I have two best friends. We've been together since elementary school, and most times we get along fine. Some of our other friends say we're like sisters. If one of us has a problem, we try to help. At least this is how it was before. We are all on the junior varsity cheerleading squad for football and basketball. At the beginning of each season, we pick a new captain for that season. It's usually no problem, but this time both of my best friends thought they should have been captain, and when neither of them got it, they got mad at each other. They said some rotten things about each other, and now they don't speak at all.

I tried to talk to both of them so they'd stop fighting. I told them it was stupid for them to be ignoring each other, and they both got mad at me. Now they won't speak to me either.

—In the Middle and Upset.

Cheerleading Causes Rift among Friends

Dear In the Middle and Upset,

The way your friends have interpreted your efforts is not right and not fair. You are in the middle, and you have good reason to be upset. I doubt that all is lost, however, and this experience will teach you a valuable lesson.

Chances are that your friends will not choose to end their friendship over this issue. In time, they will think better of their words and actions. When they do, they will see that you were only trying to help them. In the end, what you have done may actually strengthen your friendship. The position you have put yourself in is not an easy one. Even though this will probably not be a long-term problem, it is definitely a short-term problem to you.

Fights, arguments, and squabbles are seldom played out according to a set of right or fair rules. Since there are at least two people involved in a disagreement, there are at least two separate views of the facts and two ideas of what the disagreement is all about. Most disagreements, regardless of how simple or serious they may be, tend to follow no specific rules, but are instead confrontations where emotions can run high. When emotions run high they frequently collide, and then even simple disagreements can become major confrontations. Disagreements are often illogical and difficult for those not directly involved to understand. When you become involved in a disagreement between two other people, no matter how close you may be to them, you run the risk of finding yourself in the middle.

You can try speaking to your friends about other things and wait for them to cool off, or you can try to get them together and explain that their friendship means a great deal to you and that you were only trying to help them get beyond the disappointment of not being cheerleading captain. If you are unable to do this, perhaps ask your cheerleading advisor or guidance counselor for help.

My guess is that this will work out. However, until it does, you must accept and deal with the fact that in trying to help you have become involved.

Hey, Mr. McRay,

One of my teachers is really giving me a big problem. She doesn't like boys or men. She had an ugly divorce when my sister had her two years ago. She's always making dumb jokes about men, and saying how much better women are than men. I don't mind that so much, but she doesn't call on the guys in class, and she gives the girls advantages on tests. Some of the girls admit this.

We said something to her about it one time, and she got all huffy with us. She accused us of ganging up on her because a group of us went to talk to her. She said if we had a problem, we should see her one at a time. Well, because of how she acted the first time, none of us wants to be the one to go and try to tell her again. What she does in class is not fair. Even the girls say it is kind of weird.

—The Guys

Coping with a Teacher Who Is Unfair

Dear Guys,

If half of what you are saying is true, you have every reason to be angry with your teacher. There is no reason for her to favor any group of students over another. There is no place for such conduct in education. If your teacher did go through an "ugly divorce," in her mind she may have been unfairly treated by her ex-husband, but that gives her no right to be "ugly" to the young men she is teaching. She has an obligation to try to meet the needs of all of her students fairly. If she is either unable or unwilling to do this, you can either tolerate the unfair treatment or do something about it.

As I often advise, the best first step is to talk directly to your teacher. She may have been uncomfortable addressing this issue with a large number of students, so it might be wise if just two or three of you asked to see her. Keep in mind that she may not be as aware of her unfair treatment of the boys in her class as you are. She may be treating you unfairly without realizing it.

Find an opportunity to speak with her in private. If your teacher agrees to meet with you, you can address the various points you mentioned in your letter. Avoid accusing, rude comments or becoming angry. Be calm, know what you want to say, and be prepared to listen to what she says in response. By dealing directly with your teacher, you avoid blowing the matter up any bigger than it is, and you avoid involving others in a situation that is between you and your teacher. This can make it much easier for all of you to work things out. If your teacher won't agree to talk with you and your friends about how you feel, you might speak with a counselor. One of the administrators in your building or your parents may also be able to provide additional advice.

In either case, you will get support for your efforts to work through this problem. Equal and fair treatment is a basic human right. Once you are certain you are being treated unfairly, you owe it to yourself to protect your rights.

Hey, Mr. McRay,

We have this new student at our school, and she's having trouble making friends. She didn't start the year with us, and she tells us all these stories about the school she was in before—how popular she was and how many boyfriends she had. She said she played field hockey and was really good. We asked her to go out for it, but she said she hurt her ankle and was going to sit out this season.

She's always talking about how rich her parents are. She said the house they moved into is temporary because they're building a really big house. We think she's lying most of the time and she's boring. Most of us are fed up with her. How could we get her to quit lying? I want to help her.

—Yours, Fed Up

New Student's Stories Are Hard to Believe

Dear Fed Up,

The new student you refer to is in a difficult position, in unfamiliar surroundings and associating with unfamiliar people. This is not an easy transition to make at the beginning of a school year, and it's even more difficult in the middle of a year. The only things that are familiar to her are her former school and the experiences she had there, so it's only natural she would want to refer to them. She is beginning to make the transition from the old school to her new one, and she is giving you and your friends an opportunity to get to know her. These are important steps she needs to take, but the student you describe seems to be having some trouble with the truth.

I won't attempt to justify lying, but I'd like to try to explain it in this case. Maybe the new student *was* very popular at her last school; maybe she *was* a good field hockey player; and maybe her parents *are* building a large home. She may be telling the truth. If, on the other hand, she is stretching the truth, maybe she is doing so to try to win your approval. Could she be trying to win you as friends by trying to impress you? If this is her motive, it seems to be unsuccessful. She may also be feeling inadequate in her new school setting and is trying to strengthen her self-confidence by enlarging some of the details of her past. But if she is telling lies, they won't help her to form solid, lasting friendships.

If you choose to confront her directly with details on specific stories she has told, it would make it more difficult for her to make friends. A better approach, if you would like to help her adjust, might be to simply include her in your circle of friends. Don't ask too many questions about her past until she has had a chance to make some friends with whom she feels comfortable. Then she will have less reason to lie.

If the lies or exaggerations continue, take a more direct approach if you want to help her. Say that some of her stories are difficult to believe, though I'd suggest you don't make specific references. Tell her she doesn't have to try to impress you to be your friend. Tell her you just want to get to know her for the person she really is. This won't be easy for either of you, but you will be doing her a big favor in the long run.

Hey, Mr. McRay,

My daughter, a middle school student, shared a concern with me. A boy in her class acts very strange at times. She said he's always been different, (she called him odd), but he is getting worse and she's afraid. Because he's different he gets picked on, or he overhears disparaging comments intended for him to hear. Sometimes he ignores it, but other times he flies into a rage and screams at the students making fun of him. She said he seems angry almost every day, sometimes so angry that he beats his fists against walls. One time he stuck a pencil through the face of every kid he didn't like in their class picture, then wrote "I hate you all" on the bottom of the picture.

He has said several times that he's going to make everyone sorry someday. My daughter said he controls his anger when a teacher or other adult is around, so he doesn't get in trouble. She also told me that students have gotten used to his outbursts, or they laugh at him, but I think such a child needs some careful handling. Do you agree? As a concerned parent, should I get involved?

—A Very Concerned Parent

Student's Rage Is a Reason to Intervene

Dear Concerned Parent,

Everyone gets angry from time to time, occasionally even *really* angry. However, a repeated pattern of intense anger coupled with acts of self-harm and threats toward others indicates that there is indeed a serious problem. You have good reason to be concerned. If and how you get involved is up to you, but I do have some suggestions.

Since your daughter shared her concerns with you, she wants you to know. By sharing she may be asking you to do something. Ask her if she wants you to get involved. If she does, ask her for some suggestions. Your decision about getting involved should not rest solely with your daughter, but discussing this issue with her will help you get a better feel for just how serious this situation might be.

Certain adolescent and teen issues are best handled by the kids themselves. There are times when adult involvement complicates matters and frustrates teens as they seek to understand and find solutions to their conflicts and problems. Conversely, there are issues, concerns, and problems for which few, if any, teens are prepared. Such instances require responsible adults to get involved. I believe this is one of those instances.

You could go directly to this boy's parents, if you know them and feel you have enough rapport to share what your daughter has told you. They may appreciate your initiative and begin the process of getting their son some help, or they may not appreciate your involvement. Going directly to his parents could put you in a very difficult position. They may ask what right you have to suggest that something is wrong with their son, or why you feel the need to get involved in their lives. They may challenge your daughter's integrity, questioning the validity of what she has shared with you.

I suggest contacting a counselor or administrator at school. Do not attempt to diagnose, label, or define the angry boy based only on what your daughter shared with you. Instead, simply pass on the information she told you. The person you speak with may already know a lot about the boy and may be reluctant to reveal anything to you, so I advise against asking any questions. You and your daughter will have to decide ahead of time if you are comfortable with that counselor or administrator, following up by asking her additional questions.

There is a fine line between appropriate and inappropriate involvement in this situation. Over-involvement could create an uncomfortable situation for your daughter, her classmates, the boy's family, and you. No involvement could result in a tragedy of the first magnitude that could involve any number of people. Simply stated, you need to get involved, but wisely.

Hey, Mr. McRay,

There's a real problem at our school, and I'm sort of in the middle of it. There were some doors ripped off of some lockers in the freshman hall. No one has been able to find out who did it. Because it was in the ninth grade hall, the freshmen are not allowed to go on our field trip until someone confesses, or someone tells who did it.

I was in the building for a yearbook meeting after school, and I saw who did it—some tenth grade boys. They saw me and said if I told they would make me pay. I haven't told anyone, not even my parents. I don't think it's fair that my whole class is going to get punished for something we didn't do. But I don't want to tell either because I know these guys will be looking for me. I wish I hadn't seen anything. What can I do to get out of this?

—Keeping Silent

In the Middle of a Dilemma

Dear Keeping Silent,

It has often been said, "Silence is golden." In this case, I'm not sure this old saying is true. The position you are in is very complicated, and it's easy to understand your difficulty in deciding what to do. In an effort to keep from being identified and punished for the damage they caused, the boys who vandalized the lockers have intimidated you into silence. Your fear of "paying" if you tell is keeping you silent, and your silence is protecting them. All the while, the members of your class are being punished for something they did not do. You are being punished as well because of the internal conflict that you are dealing with.

My advice is to tell someone what you saw, and to do it as soon as possible. At the same time, make someone at your school aware of the threats the sophomore boys made toward you. This is not going to be easy to do, and they may attempt to bother you. However, if you do nothing, you are allowing them to make you and your whole class "pay" for what they did. And you will continue to have the internal conflict that is frustrating you now.

I suggest that you not make a big deal out of telling what you saw. This should not become an opportunity for you to make a hero of yourself. Instead, simply make someone—an administrator, counselor, or teacher—aware of what you saw. Then you have done your part to solve this problem.

As you go through life, you'll undoubtedly find yourself in situations like this again, with very similar decisions to make. Do you tell what you know and risk some reprisal, or do you say nothing and people go unpunished for misdeeds? Worse yet, do you say nothing and let innocent people be punished for something they had nothing to do with? By sharing what you know, you will be taking a stand, protecting innocent victims, and protecting your personal integrity.

Hey, Mr. McRay,

I'm going to a new school and it's rough. I'm all by myself. A lot of the kids, both boys and girls, belong to clubs. They are not really clubs they are more like gangs. If you're not in a club, you don't have any friends. Kids at my old school said this would be a tough school and I'd have to protect myself. I was scared for weeks before we moved.

I have to walk home, and I hate it every day. No one has bothered me yet, but I don't want anyone to. I'm trying not to make this a problem for my parents because they have enough to do with the move and all. So I would feel safer, I put a knife in my backpack. It worked. I am not as scared as I was without it. I don't want to hurt anyone; I just don't want to get hurt. I know you're going to tell me that I shouldn't carry a knife, but I didn't know what else to do. I have faked that I was sick just so that I wouldn't have to go to school. I'm tired of this, but I can't think of what I should do.

—Signed, Doug

Concealed Weapon More Danger Than Security

Dear Doug,

You are absolutely right—I am going to tell you that carrying a knife is a mistake. Besides being a mistake, it is illegal to carry a concealed weapon. A knife is not the answer to your problem. There are several alternatives to consider.

The first thing you must do is get rid of the knife. Carrying a knife actually creates more danger for you. Weapons create a false sense of security. By carrying a weapon, whether a knife, gun, or something else, you send conflicting messages. To some people you are saying that you are fearful, while to others you are issuing a challenge. Neither of these is the message you want to send.

After getting rid of the knife, you must talk with your parents. If they don't know how you feel about school, there is no way they can help you. It may seem to you that they have a lot on them, but I believe they can and will find time to address your concerns. Let them know that you have carried a knife to school. They may punish you for having done so, but they need to know how you feel and how you've tried to handle your fears. I would also suggest that you talk with a counselor or the principal at your school. Again, they cannot help you if you do not share your concerns.

You wrote that your new school is supposed to be tough and that you were fearful before you ever started, but you said no one has bothered you. Ask yourself how many of your fears are real, and how many are based on what you have heard or what you think might happen. It may be that a lot of your fears are more imagined than real. Starting into a new school can be difficult under the best of circumstances. If you are fearful and concerned for your safety, it would be even tougher to get started.

Once you've gotten rid of the knife and talked with your parents and someone at school, try relaxing a little. Give yourself a little more time to find a place for yourself at your new school. Once you start to make some friends, you won't feel all alone. Begin paying more attention to what you experience at your school, rather than what others tell you about it. What you find may be a pleasant surprise. However, whatever else you decide to do, GET RID OF THE KNIFE!

Hey, Mr. McRay,

Two kids in my senior communications skills class have been suspended for sending pornographic e-mails to each other.

Everybody at school has an e-mail address and access to the Internet. There are some kind of blocks on the Internet and sites we can't get to, but people can still put anything they want into an e-mail. The two kids have also lost their computer privileges for the remainder of the school year. I have to admit I've seen worse than what they wrote, but I guess that's beside the point. This sent a shock wave through the school.

We are all questioning things that we may have sent. Everyone is being very careful about their e-mail now. But if someone wanted to send you something to get you in trouble how could you stop it?

I feel like I'm at the mercy of anyone who has my e-mail address. Do you know of any way to prevent this from happening?

—Samantha

Judgment Needed for E-Mail Use

Dear Samantha,

I'm no computer expert, but from the little I know about computers and e-mail, it is rather easy to determine if material in your computer or on your computer's files and disks has been sent by you, or if it has been received from someone else. Just as is true with other forms of personal communications, such as a phone call, a letter or a note someone would pass to you, you have little real control over what comes to you. For example, if someone wants to make an obscene telephone call to you, there is little you can do to stop it initially. The same is true of a letter sent to you or a note passed to you.

Even though the Internet and e-mail are to a large extent unregulated, there are a number of things that you can do to distance yourself from questionable materials such as those that are sexual in nature, racially derogatory, or violently oriented. If someone sends you something that is offensive, let the sender know that you do not want future e-mails of that nature. You can either do this in person or by responding to the e-mail. You should also let a teacher or principal know. They can and will support your efforts to avoid such e-mails. If you do nothing, chances are you'll continue to receive them.

Forwarding items that you receive is another way of sending a broad message about the type of e-mails you feel are appropriate. It is easy to forward e-mails, even though you are not the originator of the item. Avoid sending on messages you don't approve of. It's a little like gossip—if you wouldn't say it, and wouldn't want others to think you said it, don't pass it on.

You may also want to exercise greater discretion in the Internet sites you go to. It is my understanding that many sites track their visitors and can identify them electronically. It only stands to reason if you visit questionable sites, you are more likely to get some questionable e-mails in return.

Finally, be selective when giving out your e-mail address. Certainly, e-mail addresses are not difficult to obtain, particularly if they are published in a student directory, or if they follow a simple pattern such as first initial followed by last name, followed by a common ending. However, it is still wise to avoid giving out your address to people who you feel may generate e-mail you don't want.

Your concern is a real one and one that many people must consider. No, you do not have total control over what e-mail comes to you. However, you do have control over e-mails that you generate, e-mails that you forward to other people, Internet sites you visit, and individuals to whom you give your e-mail address. I suspect that in the future, there will be more sophisticated means for controlling e-mail, but for now it does seem to be a rather wide open means of communicating, where decency and appropriateness are determined by individual preferences and personal values.

Hey, Mr. McRay,

I'm a high school senior and I guess you could say I'm very busy. I'm not complaining, because I like the things I do. I'm a member of the student council; I'm a class officer; I'm the school's representative to the Chamber of Commerce; and I play two sports. Most times I'm able to get everything done I'm supposed to do, but sometimes I get confused or forget something, like I won't get to where I'm supposed to be.

I missed a Chamber of Commerce breakfast because I overslept, and I was late for a class meeting because I just forgot about it. The teacher who takes us to the Chamber of Commerce meetings is also our class advisor. She said she was disappointed and maybe I was trying to do too much. I don't want to give up the things I'm involved in, but I don't want to be labeled irresponsible either. Should I drop out of some of the things I'm in?

—Truly, Angel

Teen Needs to Get Organized

Dear Angel,

The comment your teacher/advisor made is not one to ignore. You may well be involved in more than you can handle. Failure to meet obligations is a good indication of being involved in too much. Poor organizational skills can also make it difficult for you to fulfill obligations and meet commitments.

You overslept for the breakfast and forgot to go the class meeting. This means either you have little interest in the Chamber of Commerce and your class, or you didn't organize your schedule to allow for these meetings. In organizing your daily schedule, you must first include those things that have your primary commitment and interest. Otherwise, your participation is simply left up to chance. Maybe you'll remember to go, and maybe you won't. As you already know, such a haphazard commitment may lead some to see you as being irresponsible.

As you get older, your schedule will probably include more and more activities that call for a greater degree of commitment. Lessons in personal time management and organization that you learn now will pay dividends for many years to come. If you don't already do so, you would be wise to develop a daily pocket calendar for yourself. Carefully record meetings, engagements, and other activities. By keeping an accurate, ongoing calendar, you are more likely to avoid conflicts. But for it to be of benefit, you must refer to it daily. This way you can plan ahead, and be aware of time commitments you have made.

If, after carefully organizing your personal schedule, you still find you miss meetings and fail to fulfill obligations, you need to consider two things. Are you involved in too much, and are you sincerely interested in everything you do? If you find you are involved in too much, you will have to choose that which is most important so your participation will be meaningful. If you find you fail to meet obligations because of a lack of interest, reconsider if you want to be involved at all. A position such as class officer requires a great deal of time and energy. If you are not willing to devote the time and energy, someone else deserves a chance to serve.

That you're concerned about this and want to find a positive solution is a very good indication of your responsibility. Reconsider your time commitments, plan a daily schedule for yourself, and don't hesitate to make adjustments if that becomes necessary. It's better to limit your activities than to be a careless participant.

Hey, Mr. McRay,

Two weeks ago our student council had to raise money for some charities. We had made several pledges but didn't have enough money to pay for them. The student council president had the idea that we should have a bake sale. She gave everybody jobs to do but didn't do anything herself—not even come the day of the sale. She said she had something else she had to do and couldn't change her plans.

At an assembly two days ago, the principal recognized all the clubs that had fulfilled their pledges. He made a big point that the student council had held a special bake sale to raise what we had promised. He called the president up on the stage, congratulated her in front of the whole school, and let her talk. This girl said that the student council had made a promise and that we were going to keep it no matter how much work it took. She made it seem like she really had done something. Two guys, three other girls, and I did all of the work, and we stayed all day. We didn't get a single bit of recognition for what we did. I think that's unfair because if we hadn't gone, there wouldn't have been a bake sale at all.

Maybe I am being petty, but that hurt me. I've even thought of quitting the student council. The others who were at the bake sale are angry too. They think it's unfair we got no credit at all. What do you think?
—Sincerely, Danielle

Volunteering Should Be a Reward in Itself

Dear Danielle,

When you do something for charity, there should be little concern for the credit, recognition, or praise you receive. Doing volunteer work and helping to fulfill a pledge made by your student council should be a reward in itself. Knowing that you have done your part should generate some internal feelings of accomplishment and pride.

However, I can understand that your feelings were hurt seeing someone accept praise for the work of others. You also feel some resentment because you and the others who made the bake sale a success deserve the praise. Your leader had an obligation to recognize the service provided by the members of the council. She failed to fulfill this obligation.

To deal with your feelings, start by reconsidering your initial reactions. If being part of the student council and helping meet the council's pledges is enough for you, just drop the matter. But if you still feel as you did initially, do something about it. Share with the council president that you and the others who made the sale a success feel your efforts were unrecognized. She may respond by ignoring your concerns, by explaining why she did what she did, or by acting to correct the situation. Depending on her response, you can decide if you want to talk to the student council advisor or the principal. Regardless of what happens, you should be pleased with yourselves and the effort you put into helping your student council succeed.

Hey, Mr. McRay,

I asked a girl to the prom, and now I wish I hadn't. I didn't ask her because I liked her, or because we were going together. I just asked her so I would have someone to go with. I'm a senior and didn't want to miss the prom. Since I asked this girl to the prom I have met someone else. We started going together, and I asked her to the prom. I had to tell the first girl I couldn't take her. She didn't seem angry when I told her, but some of her friends have been giving me a rough time. She doesn't speak to me, and when I tried to talk to her, she just brushed me off. I guess I made a mistake.

—Yours, Jerry

Senior Boy Asked the Wrong Girl to the Prom

Dear Jerry,

You need not guess—you made a big mistake. A prom is not like a date or a party. A prom is a major event that most students look forward to for years. Inviting someone to a prom, then backing out to take someone else is both cruel and rude. When you invite someone to a prom, you have made a commitment for that evening. The person you invited had certain expectations. When you backed out you destroyed her expectations. This was thoughtless on your part. Since you have already asked a second girl to go, it's going to be difficult to correct this mistake. However, there may be some things you can do to lessen the effects of your error.

The first girl is probably wondering why you changed your mind. She may be concerned that she did something to cause you to back out. She may have feelings of hurt pride and self-doubt. Try reversing the situation. If she had changed her mind about going with you so she could go with someone else, what would be going through your mind?

Speak truthfully with the first girl you asked. Lying will only make the situation worse. Explain the situation you found yourself in. Do not offer it as an excuse, but instead offer it as a reason. If you agree you made a mistake, you need to tell her that. This won't be easy, but in this situation, I think it's necessary. I don't think you intentionally set out to hurt the first girl you asked, and it is important that she knows that. By explaining the situation and admitting that you made a mistake, you may reduce any feelings of self-doubt that she is wrestling with. An apology, even though it will not right this wrong, may help to mend the hurt feelings you have caused.

In this experience there is a major lesson for you. A commitment to another person carries certain obligations. If you fail to meet those obligations, you show little respect or regard for the other person. When you fail to respect others and consider their feelings, you are acting recklessly and irresponsibly.

Hey, Mr. McRay,

My math teacher has set up a system of student tutors, which he calls our "peer tutors." He said that sometimes you can learn something better from another student than you can from a teacher. If we're having trouble in math, we can get help during a study hall. There are usually at least two math tutors in each study hall, but in my study hall there's only one. My problem is the math tutor in my study hall is a girl I like. She's very nice, and we've been friends ever since we were in elementary school.

I know I could really use some help with math, and she could help me, but I don't want her to think I'm stupid. My grades in math are okay, but they could be better. I could go to my teacher, but I'd have to see him before or after school. If you were having trouble with math, and you could get help from a girl you liked, what would you do?

—Mark

Asking for Help Is a Smart Thing to Do

Dear Mark,

Asking someone for help does not mean you are stupid. In fact, asking for help is a smart thing to do. It shows you are mature enough to know your current limitations. Very few people are able to go through life without occasional assistance from others. Life is just too complex for us to be able to handle all our own needs and deal with all our own questions and problems. The young lady you are interested in obviously agreed to be a tutor, which means she has concern for others who are having trouble in math and wants to help them.

Your ability in math, or anything else for that matter, should not affect the way others view you as a person or how you see yourself. Everyone has shortcomings and weaknesses. A man who tells you he has no weaknesses does not know himself very well. Weaknesses are nothing to be ashamed of. Instead, they should be seen as excellent opportunities for personal growth.

Your math teacher's thinking is supported by a great deal of contemporary education research. Students often learn more effectively when working with another student than they can working with a teacher in a classroom setting. It's nice to know that teachers are providing opportunities for students to learn from each other. Your teacher is offering you such an opportunity.

If you choose to work with one of the peer tutors, do it with a positive attitude. Seize the opportunity to improve your math skills, and enjoy the chance to work with a friend. By so doing, you will be better able to address your current academic needs and reduce potential shortcomings. If you choose not to work with the peer tutor in your study hall, make sure you find another source of help. Consider getting help from one of the other tutors before or after school. If this is not possible, don't hesitate to contact the teacher. Explain your quandary, but make sure you get the help you need.

Hey, Mr. McRay,

The last time the SAT was given, I took it with some of my friends. During our last math section, we saw one of the guys cheating. He was using a wristwatch calculator, and the teacher told us that we couldn't use calculators. We didn't say anything then, but now we think we should have. If you'd seen someone cheating on a test, what would you do?

Sincerely,

Mindy

Should You Report a Cheater?

Dear Mindy,

It has been years since I took a math test, but I still remember how angry I was when I saw the student in front of me copying answers. I knew the girl he was copying from, and, believe me, he was getting good answers. At the time I did nothing about it, and, like you, I later thought I should have. Since then, I have seen many people cheat in many different situations. Each time I felt angry. I felt as if they were cheating me by gaining an unfair advantage. However, over the years I have learned that dishonesty carries its own unique forms of punishment.

If life were totally fair, liars, thieves, and cheaters would always get caught, and they would always be punished. However, life is not always fair, at least not immediately or obviously. There are times when dishonest acts are not detected, and they seem to go unpunished. For many people. this is frustrating because it violates their sense of fair play, and they see someone getting away with something that is not right or fair. However, even though life may not be fair on a minute-to-minute or even day-to-day basis, there is a long-term fairness about life. This long-term fairness takes many forms and is the ultimate punishment for the dishonest among us.

We are frequently able to fool those around us, but we can seldom fool ourselves for long. The person you saw cheating on the SAT may have fooled the person monitoring the test, but he certainly didn't fool himself. Cheating on a test generates a false sense of accomplishment and with it a false sense of security. Tests are an indication of acquired knowledge and academic skills. They are not only used to determine grades, but also as an indication of needed help. Cheating hides such needs by camouflaging problems. If the person you saw cheating needs help, his score may give no indication of this need, and no help will be offered.

Questioning whether you should or should not have done anything is no longer important. Some people feel it is their duty to get involved when they see things happen that they feel are dishonest, wrong, or unfair. Others choose to remain detached, allowing those involved to deal with the problem. The choice to get involved or not is yours alone.

Hey, Mr. McRay,

Being a member of a school student council is not easy. Each year it gets harder to get people to run for council. So many kids complain about the activities the council plans that it seems no one wants to get involved.

Most of the people who complain and make fun of the activities we plan never lift a finger to help. Sometimes I think they come to a dance or party so they can complain and say mean things about us. They make it harder for us to do what we plan to do, and they cause other kids not to get involved. It isn't fair. If they don't want to be involved, they should just leave us alone. We have tried to think of ways to build up our student council, but so far we have not accomplished very much. We had to cancel our last dance because not enough kids signed up to attend.

—A Student Council President

It's Impossible to Please Everyone

Dear Mr. or Ms. President,

You are right! It is not pleasant for anyone to feel his or her efforts are unappreciated. The frustrations you feel have caused many highly motivated leaders to lose their desire and want to give up. Most leaders who find themselves in this spot, regardless of the size or type of group they lead, tend to listen too intently to their critics. Their level of motivation ebbs and flows with the mood of their critics or those who have no real concern for the welfare of the group.

Your student council is one part of a larger organization—your school. Even though the student council may be a very important group within the school, it cannot stand alone. With this in mind, I'd suggest you discuss your concerns with the school administration and some of your teachers. Seek their suggestions.

One of the basic difficulties with any group that has a few people representing many is that frequently only a few feel as if they are involved. Have you tried to get other students to help plan and carry out various activities of the council? Generally speaking, personal involvement in group activities leads to some level of "ownership" and a sense of belonging. It's often easier to plan and do things yourself, rather than to motivate others, but an important quality of leadership is the ability to motivate others to get involved. Explore some ways to allow a greater number of students to take part in planning activities.

Just because you are the president of your student council, you need not—and in fact you should not—take comments about the council and its activities personally. Yes, you are a key figure in the leadership of the council, but you are not responsible for all of the council's failures, just as you are not responsible for all of the council's successes.

For the student council at your school to be successful, you don't need 100 percent involvement for all its activities. This is never going to happen. You can't please everyone, so don't let some critics destroy your commitment and motivation!

Hey, Mr. McRay,

How can you escape from a bad reputation? I guess you could say I've always been the class clown. I always have some wisecrack. I'm always picking on someone, and I've never been serious about anything.

The kids in my class think I'm funny when I'm cutting up, but I really don't have any friends. I've always done and said things to make them laugh because I thought that would make them my friends, but it hasn't worked. Lately I've been trying to be more serious about school. Last month I went out for basketball, and the first thing the coach said was that he didn't want any of my goofing around during practice or games. I hadn't done anything, and he said that. Am I a hopeless case or what?

—Signed, Woody

It's Never Too Late to Change Your Reputation

Dear Woody,

No! You are not a hopeless case—there's no such thing! Each of us, in our own way, attempts to get along in this world. In doing so, we develop personalities that are a mixture of numerous emotions, feelings, and sensitivities.

The reputation you seem to have made for yourself is not cast in concrete. It can be changed if you're willing to change it. You must understand that when you try to change a reputation, you are really trying to change the way people know you, and that is not easy. Some of the people in your class may not want to see you change. If you change, they will have to alter the way they deal with you.

A reputation, either good or not so good, is generally not made in a day, and generally cannot be changed in a day. As is true of most changes you will make in life, do not look for immediate results.

You have already identified a change you'd like to make. Now you must plan a course of action, and work your plan. The first thing to do is identify those actions that have won you the reputation as class clown, and begin to avoid or change those behaviors. When you might previously have made a smart remark, practice saying nothing. Be patient with yourself because any long-term behavior change takes time. And be patient with your friends; they won't be willing to give up easily their image of you as class clown. Prove to your teachers you wish to be taken seriously by asking serious questions and doing your work thoroughly.

A final word of caution: Just because too much humor has created some problems for you, it doesn't follow that no sense of humor at all will solve them. Don't lose your sense of humor!

Hey, Mr. McRay,

   At my school the principal announces a Student of the Week every Friday. Last week I was selected because I got an award at a YMCA swim meet. At least I think that's why I was picked. The principal had the newspaper article on the board outside the office. The next week I really got teased and picked on. Some kids I thought were my friends said some really stupid things to me. It made me wish I hadn't been picked, and it made my award seem dumb. I never got picked on before, and it makes me wish the principal had never given me an award. I didn't win. I lost!

—A Loser

Achievement Doesn't Make Someone a Loser

Dear Winner,

Sometimes when you win, you feel as though you've lost. But that does not make you a "loser." Unfortunately, the things we do or accomplish that bring positive recognition from some people will bring negative reactions from others. Your swimming award and being selected as Student of the Week deserve positive recognition, and you shouldn't allow thoughtless comments from some of your peers to make you feel like a loser. I doubt that all your peers are making negative comments and teasing you. Try to concentrate more on the positive comments you have received, and pay less attention to the teasers.

There are many reasons why some of your peers try to make your positive accomplishments look negative. A common one is jealousy. They may be jealous of you as a person, or jealous of what you've been able to do and the recognition you're receiving. Jealousy is a powerful human emotion that is difficult to define and sometimes impossible to understand or control.

Others who make fun of individual awards and personal accomplishments do so because they don't appreciate or understand their significance. They also don't know how much effort some people devote to things they are interested in. For example, those who are teasing you may simply not know how much time and effort you put in to prepare for the swim meet. They don't appreciate your efforts, and they don't understand why swimming is important to you. It's easy to make fun of something you don't understand.

Consider also that some people find it difficult to give compliments. They want you to know that they are aware of what you've accomplished, but it is difficult for them to give a personal compliment—perhaps because they've never gotten compliments themselves. Instead, they "compliment" you with some teasing comment, not intending to hurt your feelings or cheapen what you have done. Teasing is just their way of saying "good job!"

Regardless of why some of your peers are teasing you, don't make too much of it. Don't allow some teasing or negative comments to take away from the personal accomplishments you have made. Maintain a positive attitude about yourself, and continue to strive for personal achievement, even if some of your peers tease you. And above all, don't label yourself a "loser" because of some teasing. There will always be someone happy to rain on your parade. However, as your own personal parade master, only you will determine if the parade is to be canceled because of a little rain!

Mr. McRay,

    The guidance counselor at my school has really made a problem for me. When my parents went in for my sophomore conference, she said I was doing well in my classes. I am not a behavior problem, but the counselor thinks I'm a loner. I don't know why she said that, but now my parents think I'm having trouble in school and I'm not. I'm in the computer club, and I run track. I go to school activities when I want to, and I get invited to parties like everyone else. I don't have any trouble getting along with the kids in my class, and they don't ignore me or treat me bad. I like to fish and hike on weekends. Sometimes a friend might go along, and sometimes I just go by myself. I can have a good time either way. I don't have one best friend or one special group of friends.

    Since the conference, my parents have really been bugging me. They want to know if I'm having trouble in school and not telling them. They keep asking if I'm being picked on. I've tried, but I can't make them understand that I am happy in school. What can I do to make them know I'm happy just the way I am?

—Sincerely, Ethan

Labels Don't Do Justice

Dear Ethan,

Your counselor really did you and your parents a disservice. She has created a serious concern for your parents and put you in a difficult position, all with a single word. It's only natural your parents would be concerned over the counselor's comment. No parents want to think their child is being ignored, mistreated, or simply does not fit in. This is what the word "loner" means to your parents. After reading your letter, it's difficult for me to imagine why your counselor would have labeled you a loner. That term, as I have always heard it used, refers to one who avoids the company of others. That doesn't appear to be the case in your situation. You are fortunate in that you can enjoy being with others, and you can enjoy being by yourself. There are many people who are unable to do this. They find little joy in their own company and seek constantly to be in the company of others.

Talk with your parents; explain your situation to them just as you did in your letter. Suggest to them that if they are still concerned, maybe they should have another chat with your counselor. Above all, don't let one comment from your counselor affect the way that you feel about yourself. Take a lesson from this situation. Labels may be a good way to identify canned foods, but they are a very poor way to identify people.

Hey, Mr. McRay,

    I know coaches are supposed to like their sport and all, but I don't think it's fair that they treat the kids who play on their teams better than everyone else. This is unfair for both boys and girls. For example, the track coach at my school is my French teacher. If you're on the track team and you ask to go to the restroom during class, you get to go. If you're not on that team and you ask, most times he just says "No."

    We've also noticed we never have tests on the day of a track meet, and we never have assignments due the next day either. One time he even said that if we won our meet, we could skip the next test. Do you think this is fair?

—Ruby

Should Student Athletes Get Special Privileges?

Dear Ruby,

No, that is not fair! An athletic program is a very important part of a school, but participating in that program should not earn individual students special treatment. If that is happening at your school, someone is putting too much emphasis on athletics.

Participating in sports provides its own internal and external rewards. The internal rewards include being a member of a team, the physical conditioning associated with sports training, the personal satisfaction of competition, and the privilege of participation. External rewards include recognition offered athletes, such as letters and other awards, plus the potential for scholarships and other opportunities to continue participating in sports while furthering an education. To me, that sounds like sufficient reward for being an athlete.

The coach you describe has a dual relationship with the students who are his athletes. It is only natural that coaches have a closer, more personal relationship with the members of their teams. They spend more time together, and the relationship that develops is naturally going to be somewhat different. To a certain degree, a better rapport between players and their coaches must be accepted. However, when that relationship or rapport results in slighting or treating students who don't participate in a particular sport poorly, then it has gone too far.

Sports have been part of the educational system in the United States since the turn of the 20th century. Almost since then, there have been people who feel that sports have no place in a school or at least that too much attention is given to athletics. On the other hand, those who support interscholastic athletics contend that sports are the single biggest source of school spirit and pride.

I share your concern. If you feel you are being mistreated or unfairly treated just because you choose not to participate in a particular sport, you have a valid concern. I suggest you share that concern with the teacher/coach whom you mentioned.

Be careful not to use one or two incidents as a universal judgment concerning the sports program at your school. I say this because I have known coaches who are tougher on the players in class than they are on other students. They demand more from their players; they expect them to meet those demands; and they will tolerate no less. Many high school graduates contend that participating in sports helped them maintain an interest in school. Sports are an important part of a well-rounded educational program.

Athletes devote a great deal of time and energy to represent our schools on the field, the diamond, the court, the track, and the mat of competition. However, they are also students who enjoy the same rights, deserve the same treatment, and must assume the same responsibilities as all other students.

Section 3

BOYFRIENDS/GIRLFRIENDS

College Plans Cause Problems with Girlfriend
Girlfriend Dislikes His Friends
Differences Can Lead to Attraction
Marriage Is Not an Escape
"Equal" Rights a Delicate Balance
"Don't Rush It!" Is Very Good Advice
Ex-Boyfriend Is Tough Act to Follow
Age Gap Means a Lot
Ending a Relationship Is Tough
No One Has the Right to Embarrass You
Clothes Do Not Make the Person
Girlfriend Is Setting Guilt Trap
Abusive Boyfriend Needs Help
Weigh Sex Decision Carefully
Consider Both Sides before Telling Friend
Girlfriend Won't Say Why She Broke Up with Him
Friends Take Sides, Turn against Others
AIDS a Grim Reality in Dating
Meeting Dates from the Internet a Bad Proposition

Hey, Mr. McRay,

My girlfriend and I are having a problem about me going to college. She's not interested in college. Her parents own a business, and she's going to work for them. For her that's fine, but I want to go to college. Every time I bring up college, she either gets real quiet or we argue. She always says the same things. She keeps saying that if I go to college, we won't last. She thinks that just because I go to college, we will break up.

I don't see it that way, but nothing I say changes her mind. The last time we talked about it, she said I had a choice—her or college. She says our lives will be so different we'll have nothing in common. Once she told me that after I graduated from college I'd want nothing to do with her. I know she's wrong, but I can't seem to make her understand.

The only time I can remember that we talked about me going to college and didn't fight was when she made me promise that I would come home every weekend and not take classes over the summer break. She said if I couldn't promise her that, we should just break up right then and not put off something that was going to happen anyway. I promised, but I think I made a mistake. Do you agree?

—Randy

College Plans Cause Problems with Girlfriend

Dear Randy,

Yes, I think making a promise to come home every weekend and not to take summer classes is a big mistake, unless you truly want to and can live by it. You don't know now what opportunities and obligations you'll have on weekends and in the summers for the next few years. Before you assume all of the blame for this mistake, I'd like to point out that she was wrong to put you in such a position. By forcing you to choose between her and college, she blocked the opportunity for you to have both, an option that you see as possible.

To help her understand your position, ask for her undivided attention and ask her to put aside her thinking long enough to consider how you feel. Explain that you have plans and that college is a big part of them. Tell her honestly how you feel about her. Explain that there is room in your life for her and college. Remind her that a college education is important to you, but that your feelings for her are not dependent on whether or not she goes to college. If your girlfriend is still unable or unwilling to reconsider the ultimatum she offered you, make it clear that *she* is destroying your friendship, not college or you.

Another thing to consider: If she becomes used to giving you ultimatums, will there be others in the future? Any time two people come together, whether in a serious relationship, casual friendship, or a business partnership, their actions affect each other. They need to be tolerant of each other and open to a free exchange for personal needs and desires, and above all there needs to be room for reasonable compromise. Without such room, opportunities to grow and develop are very limited.

Hey, Mr. McRay,

My girlfriend expects a lot from me. At first she didn't like some of my friends, and now it seems she doesn't like any of them. I can understand her getting jealous if I hang around other girls, but she gets mad even if I am only talking to some of my friends between classes. She said if I am really interested in her, I should always come to meet her.

She makes fun of my friends and will not even speak to some of them. I had to drop out of bowling club on Thursdays because she was not in it. I'm now in a silent reading club, with her and her friends. She wants me to hang around with her friends, and I don't mind that. I like making new friends. But my friends don't like how she treats them and some of the things she says. I like her, but I don't like how she's trying to separate me from my friends.

I think you're going to say I should stand up to her and tell her not to come between me and my friends, but I don't know the best way to do it. Can you help?

—Travis

Girlfriend Dislikes His Friends

Dear Travis,

You are exactly right! No one has the right to destroy your friendships and create such an uncomfortable rift for you. You are right again when you say you must stand up to her.

It sounds to me like your girlfriend is trying to control you by dominating your time. She is trying to control who you associate with by creating uncomfortable feelings within your circle of friends. She must be a very possessive person. Some people may be comfortable in such a situation, but it doesn't sound as though you are. Ignoring this matter will not make it go away. My guess is it will only get worse unless you do something about it.

It's possible your girlfriend is not as aware of her actions as you are. Before you react, make sure she understands just how you feel. In a friendly conversation, be direct and come to the point. Be specific and offer examples of what bothers you, and be prepared to listen to her. This need not be a confrontation—you want to explain yourself and allow your girlfriend an opportunity to respond. You may not agree with the way she is treating your friends, but it's important to allow her an opportunity to explain how she feels.

Human relationships are complex, and they frequently mean different things to different people. As a friendship develops, certain demands and expectations develop along with it. It's best when these demands and expectations are acceptable to both parties of the friendship.

Hey, Mr. McRay,

My boyfriend and I are from two different worlds. I don't think I've ever known two people who are so different. I talk all the time and am very outgoing. He is quiet. My mother says he is shy. My friends tell me I'm popular, and I'm involved in field hockey, cheerleading for basketball, student council, and I sing in the choir. Jay, my boyfriend, is not unpopular, but he has just one or two good friends. He's not involved in much at school.

What I can't understand is that we get along so well. I always thought that people had to have something in common for them to get along. The reason I'm concerned is that I think I'm falling in love with him. We are seniors, and we have started talking about college. We want to apply to the same college so we can be together. I'm worried that since we are so different we will never develop serious feelings for each other. I guess I'm afraid of really falling for him, then not having it work out.

—Falling in Love

Differences Can Lead to Attraction

Dear Falling in Love,

In most successful relationships, there is a great deal of give and take. In some cases this give and take is very materialistic. For example, the store owner gives you a product and he takes your money. Such an exchange fulfills the needs of both parties. Interpersonal exchanges, on the other hand, involve far more complex forms of give and take. For example, the implications of exchanging class rings are far more significant than walking into a store and buying a CD.

The differences you describe between you and your boyfriend seem to me to be surface differences. What you may not be seeing are the deeper, more meaningful similarities you share—similarities that give rise to a friendship and continue to power its growth and development. I would also point out that there is no universal law of human nature that says that for people to get along they must be similar. In fact, it's often the differences we find in others that make them attractive, interesting, and a pleasure to be around. Such differences frequently provide avenues for sharing and individual growth.

My advice is simple. Don't assume that you and your boyfriend are so different just because you have a wider circle of friends than he does or because you are more extroverted than he is. If you wish to look for similarities, look deeper, go beyond surface appearances—do you enjoy doing the same things, do you admire the same people? Two people who are exactly alike may find the company of each other boring, uninteresting, and consequently of little interest.

As you know, there are no guarantees in life. Friendships and relationships, regardless of the personalities of those involved, frequently crumble. However, just because two people have different personalities and interests, there is no reason to assume that they couldn't enjoy a relationship that would last a lifetime.

Hey, Mr. McRay,

My girlfriend, Rita, and I have been going together since tenth grade. We'll graduate this year, and I am planning to start college in the fall. Rita could go to college if she wanted to, but all she's interested in is getting married. We've talked about college, but she can't see anything but getting married. She has real trouble with her parents. They fight all the time, and she says the only time she's happy is when she's away from them. Rita said if we got married, she'd do anything to help me get through college.

I feel bad for her, but I'm not ready to get married. I'm not sure what Rita will do if we don't get married. She might not wait four years for me because she really wants to get away from her parents. I care about her a great deal, and I want to help her, but the only answer she can see is marriage.

—Signed, Andrew

Marriage Is Not an Escape

Dear Andrew,

The constant fighting between Rita and her parents is definitely a problem, but marriage is just as definitely not the solution. You and Rita obviously have feelings for each other, but are those feelings alone strong enough to support a marriage? If you were to get married now, would it be based on your love for each other and your desire to make a lifelong commitment, or would it be based on Rita's desire to get away from her parents and your desire to help?

Your wish to help Rita is noble, as is her willingness to support you through college. However, there's a big difference between a willingness to help someone and the level of personal commitment needed to establish and sustain a marriage. You and Rita have some decisions to make, and they won't be easy ones for either of you. A good starting point would be to suggest to Rita that she ask her parents to become involved in family counseling with her. Help is available for families experiencing all sorts of problems.

The interpersonal relationships within a family are very complicated. When difficulties within these relationships go on unchecked, problems develop and, over time, they usually grow worse. A marriage between you and Rita would not resolve the problems she is having with her parents. It would only provide some physical distance between her and her parents. As is true of all personal relationships, once problems have been identified, it is time to work on them, not run from them!

Hey, Mr. McRay,

My girlfriend and I have hit a snag. She is so hung up on making sure that everything is "equal" between us that our friendship has become like a game. When we go out, she insists we pay for ourselves, or we have to take turns paying. One time I tried to pay, and she grabbed the check and said it was her turn to pay. I was embarrassed because it was like she was keeping score.

She won't even let me hold a door for her, or open her door on the car. I can't understand why this is such a big deal to her. I know she's into equal rights because of some of the things she has said in civics class. She acts like I want to take away her right to vote or something! I think she's going too far. I tried to tell her, and I got a big lecture on how men and women are equal, and how men try to keep women down by doing little things for them. That's not what I was trying to do at all.

—Sincerely, Don

"Equal" Rights a Delicate Balance

Dear Don,

Your girlfriend certainly seems to be aware of human rights and the equality of the sexes. Such awareness is important in a friendship, unless it is carried so far that it threatens the relationship. Your discomfort is understandable, and you and your girlfriend will need to come to a more comfortable understanding if your friendship is to continue.

Human history is full of examples of ethnic, racial, religious, social, financial, and gender prejudice. The inequality that results from such prejudice has always been a major problem, and the lost human potential is tragic. Those who have championed various equality movements have indeed worked for the advancement of all mankind, and their efforts are to be applauded. However, there's a point at which even the best intentions don't achieve a desirable outcome. In the case of your girlfriend, her efforts have not resulted in a desirable relationship for you.

Your attempts to be courteous have obviously been misinterpreted, and simply ignoring the feelings you have will not change the relationship between you and your girlfriend. You need to actively work toward a better understanding. Going out can hardly be pleasant if you are always worried about how a simple act of kindness or courtesy will be interpreted.

You say you've talked about this before, but little has changed. Try it again, but this time zero in on specific incidents. Be candid, be open, and be prepared to listen. Explain that you have no intention of being pushy or aggressive, and that your actions are motivated by kindness, courtesy, and a desire to be friends.

You must also be patient. Maybe your girlfriend is reacting to treatment she received from another boyfriend, or she's responding to some unrealistic notions of what might happen. Take some time to work through the feelings that both of you are having. Share your feelings with her, and be receptive to her feelings.

Hey, Mr. McRay,

I have a question that's been bothering me for some time. I have gone with several guys, and every time I start to go with someone, people say, "Don't rush it." I have heard this so many times, but I never really thought about what it means.

Well, I just broke up with this guy, and I was feeling really bad. My best friend and I were talking about it. I asked her what she thought happened. She said she thought I had rushed it. I asked her what she meant, and she said she thought I just went too fast. Then she told me that she had seen me do this before. I am still not sure what this is all about, and I thought maybe you could help me. I don't go with someone unless I really like him. I don't want to be known as pushy or that I hurt people, so I want to figure this out before I go with anyone else. Can you help me with this?

—Yours, Rae

"Don't Rush It!" Is Very Good Advice

Dear Rae,

There is an old proverb that is most appropriate to this discussion: "Haste makes waste." To be sure, this advice does not apply in all situations, but in general it is a good rule to follow. Rushing a relationship means moving through the various stages of getting to know someone at a pace that makes the other person feel uncomfortable. Most relationships go through a number of stages, usually beginning with friendly informality and spending time together in very casual circumstances. Getting to know someone in a school club can lead to getting together on Saturday afternoons, for example. If those involved find the relationship to be desirable and beneficial, it will more than likely progress. Each stage of a relationship tends to increase the level of commitment, either as bonds of friendship or in a romantic relationship. But if you rush it—if you ask for more commitment than the other person is ready to give—you'll make that person uncomfortable and may scare him or her away.

"Don't rush it" is very good advice. These simple words can be applied to much of life, not just relationships. Certain situations make it necessary for us to rush. For example, firmly established deadlines can't be pushed back, and emergency incidents can't be put on hold. However, this is not the case with most things, and particularly not with relationships you will build with other people.

When two people come together in any relationship, their unique and individual characteristics also come together. This is true among friends, family members, classmates, members of school teams and groups, neighbors, co-workers, employers, and employees. The unique characteristics that make us individuals are what make the various relationships we have in life interesting and meaningful. If we all liked the same things, had the same desires, and made the same plans, life would be very simple, and interacting with those around us would be very easy. However, it would also be boring, and there wouldn't be any fun or excitement in meeting new people.

Because we are all so different, human relationships can be very complex at times. They are often difficult to establish, and maintaining them usually takes ongoing effort. Rushing into a relationship, or rushing into closeness once one has been established, is not a good way to build or maintain them. Instead, doing so usually causes the differences between the people involved to surface and collide. For example, you may have an outgoing personality, and the boy you were going with may have been more shy. Rushing him only exaggerated the differences in your personalities. He may have been interested in a casual friendship, while you were interested in a more formal relationship. Again, rushing only made this difference bigger, and soon it became a problem.

In the numerous human encounters you will have through life, taking your time will permit you to make the most of those relationships. You will have time to get to know the people around you, and they will have time to get to know you. You will be able to look at the similarities and differences that exist between you. You will be better prepared to deal with the differences, while making the most of the similarities. You will also be giving those around you time to do the same.

Life often fails to follow your plan. Instead, something much better happens, so always be prepared to enjoy and be grateful.

Hey, Mr. McRay,

My girlfriend Karen and I have been going together for two months. Everything is great with us, but I think there is a problem with her parents. Karen went with Keith for almost two years. Karen said he spent a lot of time at her house, and he was close to her parents. She said he liked being around them more than with her. She said that was part of why they broke up.

I don't think her parents like me. They always talk about Keith, and I think they compare us. They are nice to me, but they always talk about Keith. I feel like I'm competing. Karen and I have talked about this, and she said I should ignore it. I know Karen isn't interested in him anymore, but Keith is a tough act to follow.

—Signed, Carl

Ex-Boyfriend Is Tough Act to Follow

Dear Carl,

It's easy to understand why comments from Karen's parents make you uncomfortable. Feeling like you are constantly being compared to an ex-boyfriend could get old soon.

Even though there was a primary relationship between Karen and Keith, a secondary relationship developed between Keith and her parents. This is normal and even desirable. That is, unless the secondary relationship becomes so strong that the primary relationship suffers. This is apparently what happened between Keith and Karen's parents, and Karen chose to end the relationship. Karen's parents, on the other hand, did not choose to end their relationship with Keith—that end was forced on them. Now you enter the picture, and it is only natural for Karen's parents to compare you to Keith.

For example, imagine if you had a car for several years, and you were very happy with it. Then you buy a new one, and you think and talk about the new car, as it compares with the old. (I'm not implying that human relationships are the same as those between car and driver, but I think you get my point!) The old is known and becomes a reference point for the new.

Understanding why Karen's parents frequently refer to Keith may help you deal with this situation. Maybe they are just trying to be open about the good relationship they had with Keith. Or maybe they're sending you some signals as to how they would like you to act toward Karen. They may also be trying to develop a relationship with you, and they're giving you some insights about themselves. It is difficult to tell what their intentions are. However, there are several ways you can handle this situation.

The easiest way would be to acknowledge the comments, but make no more of them. Don't compare yourself to Keith. If the comments persist, try talking to Karen again. She may be willing to say something to her parents, but be careful. You don't want to create problems between her and her folks. That wouldn't do anyone any good.

You might also choose to say something directly to Karen's parents. You could answer some comment about Keith with, "You must have been very close to Keith. You refer to him quite often." Such a comment would make the point that you have noticed how often they speak of him.

Give yourself and your relationship with Karen and her parents some time. Try not to jump to any conclusions. Be secure in yourself. Just because someone is being referred to in positive terms, don't view the comments as being negative toward you. And above all, don't look at yourself as the actor who is following Keith, for if you do, you will never have top billing with Karen or her parents.

Hey, Mr. McRay,

   I am in tenth grade and will turn 16 soon. My boyfriend is 20. He graduated two years ago, and he still lives at home, but he has a good job. When I first met him my parents thought he was nice, until they found out how old he was. They won't let me go anywhere with him anymore, and they want him to stop coming to see me. They said they still think he's nice, but too old for me. Why is his age such a big deal? If you love someone, is age a problem? Who's right?

—In Love!

Age Gap Can Mean a Lot

Dear In Love!

Sorry, I am not a referee or a judge. I cannot tell you who is right or wrong. Love is a very complex emotion, and it cannot be explained as a simple right or wrong. There are, however, some simple realities that may be behind the position your parents have taken. One is that you are 16 and your boyfriend is 20—you can't change that difference in your ages. Another reality is that you are still in school and your boyfriend is not.

Ask yourself: If this is such a simple reality, why are my parents making such a fuss? Let me share some of the deeper implications with you. As you develop from childhood through adolescence and on to adulthood, you go through many changes. Your likes and dislikes will change. The things you find important will change, as will your needs and desires. When you develop a close friendship with someone who is at or near your stage of personal development, your likes and dislikes, what you feel is important, and the rights and responsibilities you enjoy will likely be similar.

On the other hand, when you enter a friendship with someone who is at a different stage of development, there will be some differences. When these differences surface, several things can happen. The relationship can fail; one person can dominate; or those involved can seek to arrive at a balance. The last of these possibilities is the most desirable, but unfortunately, broken friendships or relationships where one person dominates frequently result.

You are entering one of the most changeable periods in life. The potential differences between a 16-year-old girl and a 20-year-old man are great. If you are not able to strike a balance in your relationship and maintain it, one of you could well be drawn into situations that you are simply not ready to handle or deal with. This is probably the basis for your parents' concerns. They may be concerned that your relationship will develop so quickly that you won't finish school. They may also be concerned that your boyfriend will demand a level of personal and physical commitment you're not prepared for.

As you get older, a four-year age difference will become less significant. In ten, or even five years, such an age gap will reveal far fewer differences. I'm not saying there's no way your friendship can work, but I agree that your parents' concerns are legitimate and should not be dismissed.

Hey, Mr. McRay,

Why can't some people take a hint? Why do they try to keep something going when it is over? This guy and I went together for over a year, but we broke up almost six months ago, and I can't get away from him. I'm seeing other people, but Rob hasn't. He keeps calling me; he hangs around my locker at school; and he even followed my new boyfriend and me to the movies one night.

When Rob and I broke up, we agreed to still be friends, but now he is going too far. I've tried not to be rude with him, and I asked him to give me some space. I even tried ignoring him, and he still didn't get my message. My new boyfriend offered to talk to him, but I think that might make things worse. I wish I knew how to get him to leave me alone without hurting him.

—Frustrated

Ending a Relationship Is Tough

Dear Frustrated,

Ending a friendship or a relationship without some hurt feelings is a very difficult thing to do. In fact, I'd say it's almost impossible. Ending a relationship is even more difficult, as you have found, if only one of the people involved wants to end it. You have chosen to go on with your life, and Rob has not. In his mind, there is still something left of the relationship or friendship that you once had. Your patience and desire not to be rude or hurt him shows some real understanding on your part.

There are many reasons why people enter into a relationship, and many reasons why people end them. Human needs provide the "why" for friendships and relationships. If you could find out why Rob is having difficulty accepting that your friendship is not what it once was, it might be easier for you to get him to back off without hurting him. Having your new boyfriend talk to Rob may confuse the situation even more. Ignoring him has not delivered the message you want to send, so I'd advise against continuing that as well. Try to talk with Rob, letting him know you do not want him calling you, hanging around your locker, or following you on dates. You must tell him what you expect, and you will need to give him an opportunity to react.

Give him some time to adjust his behaviors, but if he doesn't give you the space you need, you might have to seek some help. I would assume that your parents are already aware of this matter. If they're not, explain your concerns to them before you do anything else. Depending on how this situation develops, it might become necessary for them to become involved. Your desire not to hurt Rob is admirable, but your right to get on with your life is every bit as important, and that right should be your ultimate goal.

Hey, Mr. McRay,

I'm going with a guy two years older than I am. I really like him, but I'm not sure he likes me. When we're not around his friends, he treats me great, and I like being with him. We talk a lot, and he is very considerate. But when we get around his friends, he ignores me or says rude things to me and about me. I'm embarrassed and uncomfortable around his friends. I haven't said anything to him yet because I thought it might only be my imagination, and I wasn't sure just what to say. I like him, but I don't like the way he treats me sometimes. I don't know what to do because I don't want him to drop me. What should I do?

—Uncomfortable

No One Has the Right to Embarrass You

Dear Uncomfortable,

No one has the right to embarrass you or make you feel uncomfortable. If you have such feelings, you're not in a solid relationship. In fact, uncomfortable feelings are usually a reliable indication of a problem. You have good reason to be concerned. Friendships should be based on mutual respect and concern for others, not embarrassment and social discomfort.

You should discuss your feelings with your boyfriend as soon as possible. Be honest and direct. You can't expect him to understand how you feel if you act otherwise. A good friendship is nothing to be cast aside lightly. He deserves a chance to correct the situation. He may be unaware of the way he treats you when he is around his friends.

If your boyfriend values your friendship, he won't want to embarrass you or make you feel uncomfortable. If, on the other hand, he does nothing to correct the situation once you have explained it to him, he is telling you that he doesn't value your friendship. No one likes to be rejected or dropped, but if uncomfortable feelings and embarrassment are going to be a constant part of your friendship, maybe it's not much of a friendship and should be ended.

Friendships are a valuable asset in life and cannot simply be made and forgotten. Instead, friends must be worked at. When problems arise—and they will—they must be identified, discussed, and worked on until they are resolved. You seem to have identified a problem; now you and your boyfriend must work on it together until it is solved.

Hey, Mr. McRay,

My girlfriend and some of her friends are really into the way guys dress at school. They started this last year, and now it's like a big game to them. Some of the guys in our class are hung up on this. They have changed the way they dress, and they try to get these girls' attention by how they dress. For some of the guys it's a contest to see who can dress the best. It's not a big deal to me because I think it's kind of weird and I really don't get into it.

Tabitha, my girlfriend, has started telling me how to dress. She knows what clothes I have better than I do. The last time my mom took me shopping for clothes, she went along. She picked everything I got, and that made my mom pretty mad. She didn't say anything in the store, but later she said if Tabitha was going to pick all my clothes, Tabitha could pay for them the next time!

There was a dance last Friday, and instead of having a good time we had a fight because I didn't wear what she told me to. I tried to talk to her about this, but she doesn't think anything is wrong with suggesting what I wear to school. Do you have any ideas on how to handle this?

—Wayne

Clothes Do Not Make the Person

Dear Wayne,

I've heard of girls "suggesting" what a boyfriend might wear to a dance or a party, or coordinating colors for a formal or a prom, but your girlfriend and her friends have really gone too far. You and she need to talk, and so do any of the other guys in your class who are in the same situation you are. I understand you have tried talking before. I'd try it again, and if it fails again, I'd simply ignore the efforts of your girlfriend and her friends to control how you dress.

The notion that "the clothes make the man (or the woman)" has never been a comfortable one for me. Clothes may make a statement about a person's mood, personality, and likes or dislikes, but they do not "make the person"! Even if there's a shred of truth to that statement, your girlfriend and her friends seem to think "the clothes *are* the man"!

The way a person dresses is a matter of individual choice, which is closely tied to personal freedom. When someone, for any reason, tries to dictate how another person dresses, he or she has invaded the zone of personal freedom. It sounds as if your girlfriend and some of her friends are playing a game, and you and some of the guys in your class are the players. Your discomfort with this game is easy to understand. As long as you and others continue to play, the game will continue. If you cannot solve this problem by talking to your girlfriend, simply ignore her efforts to control how you dress. Try telling *her* how to dress, asking that she wear certain clothes each day. Maybe she'll get the point. And I agree with your mom: If Tabitha wants to pick your clothes, she should be prepared to pay for them.

Hey, Mr. McRay,

I have a big problem with the girl I'm going with. I really want to break up with her, but every time I even suggest it, she goes crazy. One time she started screaming and crying at lunch. She made a real scene when she ran out of the cafeteria. I was embarrassed and afraid of what she would do, so I told her I was only kidding. Another time I said I thought we should start seeing other people, and she ran off and hid in a mall all day. When I found her, she said she was thinking of killing herself.

I want to break up now more than ever, but I feel trapped. I can't tell what she will do, and I don't want to be responsible if she runs away or hurts herself. What would you do if you were in my shoes?

—Yours, Jared

Girlfriend Is Setting Guilt Trap

Dear Jared,

If I were in your shoes, I would change shoes as quickly as possible! It's understandable that you feel trapped, and in a way you are trapped. Your girlfriend has worked you into a corner. You are caught between your wish to end an undesirable relationship and your wish not to be responsible for any rash actions she might take. Your friend has put you in a very difficult position by taking advantage of your caring nature. You don't want to see her do something foolish that could endanger her. She is aware of this, and she is using your concern to make you stay in a relationship that you want to end. She is intimidating and controlling you with your own feelings. As I am sure you already know, a friendship like this is going nowhere fast.

Based on some of her past actions, or rather reactions, you'd be wise to seek some help. Several people could help you work through this. You might want to begin with your parents. Explain the situation to them, and let them know your concerns. You might also wish to seek the help of a counselor at your school. Although this is a troublesome situation to you, your counselor has worked through similar situations and will be sensitive to your problem.

From this experience you have gained some valuable insights into one of the more unpleasant sides of human nature. In desperation, which can result from many causes, some people resort to some rather strange means or tricks to try to control a situation or another person. Your girlfriend chose to intimidate you. She literally scared you into staying with her. Human relationships, regardless of the type, must be based on mutual concern, shared consideration for each other, and an open trust. When fear, intimidation, embarrassment, or any other type of unfair emotional control surfaces, the relationship is headed for trouble.

If efforts to resolve the problem are not successful, ending the relationship should be seriously considered. Otherwise, what was once a friendship can quickly deteriorate into a confining, menacing trap that benefits no one. Sympathy, guilt, or misplaced feelings of responsibility are not good reasons to continue a friendship from which you would otherwise like to withdraw.

Hey, Mr. McRay,

     This letter is about my sister, Gina. We are very close. She says her boyfriend sometimes hits her when he gets mad. I was with them once when he hit her. I was scared, but I didn't say anything. I asked her if he had hurt her. She said not really. She said he only hits her when he gets mad.

     When she came home from school yesterday, she had a bruise on her arm. She said Eddie hit her because she was not waiting at his locker at lunch. She asked me not to tell our parents. She said she loves him, and they would not let her see him anymore. I'm scared he's really going to hurt her. I told her, but she just said not to worry. She says he'll stop when he learns to control his temper. If your sister was going with a guy like Eddie, what advice would you give her?

—A Scared Sister

Abusive Boyfriend Needs Help

Dear Scared Sister,

You have good reason to be concerned about Gina and Eddie. Whenever a person is being hit or abused in any way, there is a problem. Though Gina may seem to be ignoring this, she knows it is a problem. That's why she asked you not to tell your parents. When one person hits another, the hurt goes far beyond some physical pain. Certainly it hurts when you are punched or slapped, but the embarrassment, rejection, and anger that follow can be much more painful.

Gina has told you she loves Eddie and wants to keep seeing him. It may be difficult for you and me to understand, but Gina must have her reasons. She said she hopes Eddie will stop hitting her when he learns to control his temper. Perhaps Gina wants to give him a chance to grow up, but she should be aware that, more often than not, adults who abuse others acted the same way when they were teens and children. This doesn't mean that every boy who hits his girlfriend will be abusive to a wife some day. But abusive teens frequently become abusive adults if they don't get some help to learn more acceptable behavior toward others.

The reasons why people hit, punch, slap, or abuse others can be very complex, and they can be very difficult to overcome. Gina should not tackle this alone or in any way make herself responsible. Your parents and Eddie's parents need to know. They can be of great help and support to both Gina and Eddie. Gina is not in a position to be Eddie's total support system. She needs help if she is going to help Eddie.

Share your concerns with your sister, or give her a copy of this letter. If she doesn't already know, let's hope she will come to understand that Eddie needs more than just some time to grow up and more help than she alone can give. She will also see, or be reminded since she probably already knows, that her sister cares about her a great deal!

Hey, Mr. McRay,

I'm not asking you for an answer. I'd just like you to give me some advice so I can make up my own mind. Matt and I have been going together for three months, and we're in love. At least I think we are. We're still in high school (both seniors), so we can't be together as often as we want. When we're together, we always have a good time.

Last weekend Matt said it was time to make our relationship deeper. He said sex was a natural part of going together, and that if I loved him I would want to show him. He said that everyone our age has had sex and that it was no big deal. He said if I didn't want to go to bed with him, maybe I didn't really love him, and we should break up. I'm not a prude, but I don't want to lose him either. I'm simply not ready to be as involved as he wants. I feel trapped!

—Signed, Jyle

Weigh Sex Decision Carefully

Dear Jyle,

I cannot give you the correct answer to your problem. You are the only person who can determine how best to handle this situation. I can, however, share some rather simple advice that has been around for years. Some of what Matt told you is most definitely true. Sexual relations are indeed a natural part of loving human relations. Sexual intimacy is a beautiful way to express love, and, undoubtedly, some of your friends are sexually active. Beyond these simple points, Matt has built a trap for you from some classic sexual myths. I doubt seriously if all of your friends are having regular sexual relations. Certainly there are some who are, but just as certainly there are those who are not. The notion that "everyone is doing it" simply is not true. Even if it were true, sex is not a game to be played just because others are doing so. Sexual intimacy is a significant element of a mature, loving relationship. It *is* a big deal and should not be taken lightly.

Human intimacy becomes cheap and shallow when you are forced to use it to *prove* your love. If Matt suggests your friendship is based solely on your willingness to comply with his physical suggestions, you need to reexamine your relationship. Your uncomfortable feelings are a pretty clear indication that you are not ready for the level of physical involvement that Matt is seeking.

As you already know, sexual relations can result in some serious consequences. An unplanned pregnancy, any number of sexually transmitted diseases, undesirable feelings of guilt, and unwanted responsibilities are just a few. Although they may sound very similar, there's a great deal of difference between being a prude and being prudent. I'm sure you're not a prude, but I hope in your relationship with Matt, you take the time to be prudent!

Hey, Mr. McRay,

One of my friends is interested in this guy who is a senior. We are sophomores. He has kind of come on to her, and she thinks he likes her. I know she likes him. I think if he asks her to go out with him, she will.

The guy she's interested in lives near me. I don't know him very well, but my sister does and she says he doesn't treat his girlfriends very nice at all. Her best friend went with him, and she broke up with him because he was always flirting with other girls. I've heard that he did that to other girls, too.

I don't know if I should tell my friend what I know about him. One side of me says to do nothing and just stay out of it. The other side of me says I should share what I know. I don't want to see her get hurt, and maybe I can keep that from happening. If you were me, what would you do?

—A friend, Heather

Consider Both Sides before Telling Friend

Dear Heather,

Unless a student in your school has recently moved in from another area, chances are good that he or she is going to be known by a number of other students. You can be sure that any person who is known by others—whether a child, a teen, or an adult—will have both friends and enemies. Just as certainly, you can be sure that friends will probably have something nice to say about the person while the enemies will likely have something negative to say. These are some simple and true characteristics of human relationships.

In this case, you may not be an enemy of the guy your girlfriend wants to go out with, but you know something negative about him. Part of you wants to share that with your friend, and another part of you feels it's none of your business. (This might be the side of you that realizes that you don't know this guy very well, and that your opinion is based on secondhand information.) Before you make any decisions, think through this situation very carefully.

Drop some hints to your girlfriend before you come out and share what you have heard about him. If he does ask her to go out with him, suggest that she get to know him a little before making any commitments. You would be encouraging her to proceed with caution, but not blocking her chances to develop a new friendship.

Hey, Mr. McRay,

   My girlfriend just broke up with me last week. We weren't fighting. We didn't even have an argument. I thought we were getting along fine, but I guess something must have been wrong. When I tried to talk to her about it, she wouldn't say anything. She didn't ignore me but wouldn't talk at all about why she broke up with me. She made a lot of small talk and just kind of brushed off my questions. When I asked if she was mad or anything, she just kind of smiled and said, "No." Then I really didn't understand.

   I was embarrassed at first, and maybe more so because I tried to talk to her a second time. I feel like a jerk because maybe other people know something I don't know. I asked some of her friends, but they don't know why she broke up with me either. I'm not sure I really want to go with her anymore, but I would like to know why she wanted to break up. What would you do?

—Baffled

Girlfriend Won't Say Why She Broke Up with Him

Dear Baffled,

No one likes to be put off or taken lightly, particularly when trying to get some information. I can easily understand your embarrassment and frustration in this situation.

Not all people are willing or able to share their feelings. Some folks find it very difficult to speak what is on their minds. They may be wrestling with feelings they don't understand, or they may find it difficult to put their thoughts and feelings into words. As a result, they sometimes choose to say nothing. If this is the case with your girlfriend, you will have to give her time. Don't nag or make a pest of yourself. You have tried twice to deal with this matter, so she should make the next move.

Your girlfriend may also be playing a game with you. She may be testing to see just how serious you are about her, or she may be playing with your emotions for some reason. It's also possible she wanted to break up with you for no particular reason and has chosen to end your friendship through confusion and frustration. I'd suggest two possible courses of action. One is to wait a while and, if she doesn't talk to you about this, go to her and let her know that you have no idea why she wanted to break up. Be firm and tell her that you are willing to listen when she is ready to talk. The other course is to leave things just where they are until she comes to you. This is a decision you will have to make because only you know how you feel. Don't assume more responsibility than is necessary. You have been frank and open to this point. You found yourself in an odd situation, and you have tried to work through it. There's not much more you can do if your girlfriend is unwilling or unable to talk.

Hey, Mr. McRay,

I think I made a big mistake. My boyfriend and I had a big fight, but now we're back together again. The fight was really stupid to begin with, but we both did something dumb. When we were mad at each other, we turned our friends against each other, too. Now his friends don't like me, and most of my friends don't like him. They keep telling us we shouldn't have gotten back together. What can we do now so they'll understand we're not mad at each other any more?

—Yours, Marion

Friends Take Sides, Turn against Others

Dear Marion,

It's wonderful that both you and your boyfriend have friends who care. Such friends are often hard to come by. However, as you have found out, even the best of friends can become too close to a particular situation. Now that you and your boyfriend have solved the problems you were having, you must deal with the other people you have involved, and this won't be an easy task. You may actually have more problems clearing this matter up with your friends than you did working things out with your boyfriend.

When two people have a disagreement or a problem, it's generally those two people who must deal with it. Certainly there are times when it's wise to ask others for help, but at all times it's important to remember whose problem it is. When you involve others, they develop a certain level of "ownership" of the problem. When others, regardless of how well-intended they may be, become too close, they run the risk of becoming part of the problem. When they become part of the problem, it's more difficult for them to become part of the solution.

Speak candidly with your friends. Explain that you and your boyfriend have worked through the problems you were having. Thank them for their support. Let them know you have moved ahead and they need to do the same. Some of your friends might suggest that your problems are not over at all. They might say, "If you had problems once, you'll have problems again." This may be true, but you and your boyfriend have decided to try it again, and your friends should respect your decision. If they cannot do so, you will simply need to move on without their support.

No one can predict the future. You and your boyfriend may be at the beginning of a lifelong relationship. You may also be in a relationship that will falter again and again. Your decision to get back together will enable you to find out. If you had called it quits after your first disagreement, you would never have known. Regardless of how things work out, you will always know that you gave it a second chance. This experience can teach you that the decision to involve friends in personal problems must be evaluated carefully.

Hey, Mr. McRay,

I am a college freshman. I dated in high school, but now dating is more serious. I am meeting people from a much wider area than before. I am currently seeing just one person, and that has made it a little easier for me. We have kept our relationship very casual, and she has been comfortable with that up until recently. I am getting the sense that our friendship may become closer, and I welcome that. However, one reason I have tried to keep things casual is that I am fearful of AIDS. It is a fact of life today, and it scares me. I am concerned that our relationship will develop to the stage of intimacy, and, frankly, I don't have any idea how I will handle the AIDS issue. If we do not address it, I am going to be totally un-comfortable. I do not want to embarrass the women I am seeing, but I do not want to expose myself to AIDS either. Do have any ideas?

—Brent

AIDS a Grim Reality in Dating

Dear Brent,

There are a number of ways to approach the issue of AIDS. This is not the forum for discussing the medical issues of the AIDS epidemic. Nor is it the forum for discussing the variations of safe sex or abstinence, which is far and away the safest solution. I'll assume you are aware of these. To me, your letter and your concerns speak of the moral issue of AIDS. I would like to share some thoughts from that perspective.

You are correct that AIDS is a fact of life. It's also a cause of death, and, with that in mind, you have good reason to be concerned. Not acting on those concerns would be foolish. In fact, if you were not concerned, I would be telling you to wise up and realize the potential ramifications of your lack of concern.

Do not dismiss your fears. Instead, I suggest you work with them. If you are dating a young woman and you feel the relationship is progressing to the point of any physical intimacy, you have every reason to discuss AIDS openly and frankly. You would be foolish not to. In fact, if you don't approach the subject with her, you are sending her a message that you have little concern for either her or yourself. Although this may be an awkward portion of the evening's conversation, putting the threat of AIDS behind you is important. My guess is that the thought has crossed her mind as well.

You mentioned that you will feel uncomfortable discussing AIDS with your girlfriend. If your relationship has not yet progressed to where you can discuss AIDS, other sexually transmitted diseases, unwanted pregnancies, and related issues, then maybe sexual intimacy in your relationship is inadvisable. You'll have to answer this question yourself. Remember abstinence is a solution.

Numerous surveys have reported that AIDS is among the most critical issues and concerns of those who are dating, and it should be. The AIDS epidemic is a harsh reality. Nonetheless, with reasonable caution and frank relationships, it does not have to be a concern that makes dating seem like a walk through a minefield.

Hey, Mr. McRay,

I spend most evenings on the Net. I guess you could say I'm addicted. I enjoy it very much because it's so easy to meet people. Meeting people is not easy for me in person. In chat rooms it doesn't matter what you look like or anything like that. You can just talk to people because there is nothing to be nervous or uptight about.

I'm getting together with a guy I met on the Net for a real date. After we met in the chat room, we have talked a lot by e-mail. From what he told me about himself, we have a lot in common. One of my girlfriends thinks I'm making a mistake meeting him. I think she is jealous because I made a connection over the Net and she has not. Do you think I am making a mistake?

—Paula

Meeting Dates from the Internet a Bad Proposition

Dear Paula,

The Internet has opened a number of communication options that previously were not available. The opportunity for one-on-one "chatting" is very popular. But as you can well imagine, each of these options has its pitfalls and drawbacks. Let me explain a few of the drawbacks with Internet chatting.

Although Internet chatting is quick, easy, and one-on-one, it is also very distant in many respects. You do not see the people with whom you are chatting, you don't hear their voices; and you have little or nothing to help you determine what type of people they are or what their intentions may be. You aren't getting any of the signals that indicate whether a person is sincere or not—something you can generally pick up in person. So chatting on the Net is at the same time very personal yet very distant.

I have heard of Internet relationships that have worked out nicely. I have also heard of such relationships that turned into nightmares. I advise great caution. Ask yourself a few questions and be prepared to answer them honestly. How do you know if the person you are meeting has been honest and forthright with you about himself? What are his intentions? What are your expectations, and what are his expectations?

Going on any blind date carries certain risks, but if a friend has set up a blind date for you, you at least have the friend's recommendation for the person's character. The scenario of an Internet date raises that risk factor significantly. Neither you nor anyone you know has met this person, other than through computer messages you have shared. Many people say only positive things in order to make themselves more appealing in the chat rooms. There have been numerous stories of Internet dates that have resulted in unpleasant and even tragic consequences. It's not something to be taken lightly. Would your parents approve of your doing this?

I advise you not to go, but if you feel you must, be very cautious. Build in safety factors for yourself—meet in a highly public place like a restaurant. It would be unwise to meet at your home or his home. You may also want to suggest that you each bring a friend. If he balks at either of these suggestions, give this some more thought. If you decide to meet, don't give out more personal information until you know the person much better.

I'd like to offer another suggestion. You mention you enjoy the Internet because it allows you to relax and just be yourself, and you don't have to worry about how you look. Addictive use of chat rooms on the Internet will reinforce your self-conscious feelings about your shyness and personal appearance. Perhaps you could work on that aspect of your appearance that bothers you, which will increase your confidence with other people. If it is something beyond your control, relax and accept it.

Continue enjoying the Internet, but keep it in perspective—any kind of addiction means that you are not in control of yourself. Be careful that you do not become so dependent on the Internet to meet people that you avoid personal contacts in life. The Internet is a great research and communication tool, but it should not replace or diminish your interpersonal skills and personal contacts.

Section 4

PERSONAL DEVELOPMENT

Fear of Failure Will Limit Participation in Life
Grieving Is an Individual Process
Try to Enjoy Each Stage of Life
Heavy Drinking Is a Serious Problem
Making Tough Decisions
He Wants to Be a Nurse
If You Think Negative Thoughts, You Defeat Yourself
Five Steps for Making Decisions
Free Use of Internet Calls for Mature Judgment
Crying Is an Innate Reaction
Worry Is a Waste of Time
To Drink or Not to Drink?
Self-Esteem Is Very Complex

Hey, Mr. McRay,

There are times when I don't do things because I'm afraid I won't do them right. When I fail at something I feel horrible. I don't like feeling dumb about myself, so I have always avoided things I thought might not work out for me. This was OK, but now I have a little problem. I want to apply to be in the National Honor Society. The teachers must approve students who get in. I'm afraid not all my teachers will sign for me. My grades are good enough, and I don't know of anything any teachers have against me. I just don't want to apply and be rejected. It would be too embarrassing. I would feel really stupid if I got turned down.

My dad said I'm cheating myself. I told him that being rejected would be worse than not being in the society. I told him I'd decided not to even try. He said I was making a mistake. I'm pretty sure of what you'll say, but I still would like your suggestions.

—Sincerely, William

Fear of Failure Will Limit Participation in Life

Dear William,

If you thought I would tell you to apply for admission to the National Honor Society, you were right. You won't know if you'll be accepted until you try. Your dad's thinking is exactly like mine, and I would offer the same advice. Show me a person who has never failed or even risked failure, and I will show you a person who has never really succeeded. Failures are a part of life. Few people try to fail, and no one can totally avoid failure. A certain number of setbacks in life are inevitable; they are just going to happen. Attempting to avoid failure is a noble goal until such an attempt begins to limit participation and initiative. Let me explain.

There are many ways to limit the number of failures you must face. You can prepare for what you do in life. You can seek the help of others. You can devote your best efforts and remain with a task or project until you find some success. However, before any of these methods to limit failures can be used, you must be involved. You have chosen to limit failures by not participating. If you agree that success is the opposite of failure, you fail when you do not participate because there is no way for you to succeed. I strongly urge you to apply for admission to the National Honor Society. This is the only way you can possibly be admitted.

In life there are active participants and there are observers. There is a definite place for both, and you must decide which you wish to be. Observers meet with fewer direct failures, but they also meet with far fewer successes. Failures can be positive experiences if you let them. Some of the best lessons come from life's setbacks. I'm not suggesting that you purposely set out to fail; I'm suggesting that you try to experience life's opportunities with a little less concern for possible failures. If you do fail, learn, bounce back, and try again.

You must accept responsibility for your failures, but it's important not to let them distort your view of yourself. You will find that success is often the result of past failures. Thomas Edison, for example, once said he succeeded at inventing the first light bulb because of all the failures he'd had trying to invent it. Don't let the fear of failure limit your participation in life. Like your dad told you, you may be cheating yourself!

Hey, Mr. McRay,

My grandmother died two weeks ago. I was very close to her. She lived just down the street from our house. I stayed with her every day after school from kindergarten until I started high school. Even this last year I went there most days. I knew that she was not in perfect health, but I didn't know she was going to die. I tried to talk to my parents, but they are dealing with their own feelings. They said I will get over it in time. My mother said she thought I knew that my grandmother was not well. She is the first person close to me who has died. My friends said they were sorry for me, but it is tough to talk to them about how I feel. I'm afraid I will start to cry. I don't want to look like a baby. If I was older would this be easier to deal with?

—Angelina

Grieving Is an Individual Process

Dear Angelina,

Your grandmother's passing has made one of life's harshest realities very real for you. This is the reality of death. As unpleasant and painful as death is to the survivors, it is one of the certainties of life. As you said in your letter, your parents are dealing with their own feelings, but there is no reason why you cannot and should not talk to them about your feelings. When a family suffers a death, the strength and support that family members can offer each other is an important part of the grieving process. You might need to say specifically you need to discuss your painful feelings.

First, I would like to address your comment about crying. Crying is a natural emotional response. It's not something that you should be ashamed of, and it's very common to cry frequently when grieving. Crying is a healthy release of feelings and emotions.

When someone close to you passes on, there are various stages of grief that you will go through. Numerous psychologists and sociologists have tried to define these stages. They agree that there is no single stage that lasts a particular length of time, and that no two people grieve in exactly the same way. However, there are some gross similarities to how most of us cope with the death of someone we love. In general terms, our first reaction to the death of a loved one is shock. This is particularly true in your case since you did not realize how ill your grandmother was. In this stage there can be an uncomfortable numbness and a sense of disbelief. Then we often try to deny the finality of death, telling ourselves our loved one is not deceased but will walk in one day and everything will be as it was. Then follows a difficult period of despair as bereaved people begin to accept the fact that a loved one has passed away. In this stage there is often a deep sense of loneliness. We seek to explain, understand, and cope with the how's and why's of death. We feel a strong sense of loss as we come to realize how great an impact the death will have on us. If there are any unpleasant memories, more than likely they will surface at this time.

The final stage of grieving is recovery, and, Angelina, it does come. In time, dealing with your feelings and emotions will become easier. In this final stage, you will likely recall a host of pleasant memories and images. You will begin returning to your normal routine; you will be getting on with your life. Instead of concentrating on how a particular relationship has ended, you will focus more on how good that relationship was and the lasting impact it will have on you. The beauty of the relationship will become what is most memorable and real to you.

Talking about your feelings to your friends may not be easy or comfortable for you or them. On the other hand, you may have a friend or classmate who has gone through a similar situation and could help you deal with your feelings. You might want to talk to your guidance counselor. He or she could be a good source of support. Your counselor might be able to put you in touch with others who have had similar experiences or a student support group. I do not know what services are available at your school, but contacting your counselor is a good first step. Depending on your religious affiliations, you should also consider contacting a leader in your church.

Death is one of the harshest eventualities of our existence. I wish I could tell you that it will become easier as you grow older, Angelina, but it will not. You may have a broader understanding of death's reality as you get older, but dealing with the loss of someone you love will never be easy. I for one believe that the pain and sadness of death are a price we pay for loving others. It may be of little consolation to you now, but the pain you are currently feeling will someday seem like a small price to have paid for the happiness, joy, and pleasant memories that loving your grandmother has brought you.

Where you have been provides some insight and experience. Where you are going requires some foresight and provides an opportunity to use your experience.

Hey, Mr. McRay,

     Being 14 is no fun! I want to be older. I'm not allowed to date; I can't get a job yet; and I can't even drive. I'm too old to do kid things, and I'm not old enough to do some of the things I want to do. In eighth grade you are kind of stuck in between being a kid and being an adult. My parents keep telling me to be patient. They say I'll grow up fast enough, but I'm getting tired of being treated like a kid. I try to act mature, but no matter what I do, I'm still 14, and I still feel like a kid. I want to make more of my own decisions, and I want to be more independent. Most of my friends feel like I do and want what I want, but none of us have any answers. Do you?

—Signed, Allen

Try to Enjoy Each Stage of Life

Dear Allen,

At your age it's common to wish you were a little older. It's difficult to imagine now, but as you grow older you will probably experience some opposite feelings—you will wish you were a little younger. However, age is simply one of those things that is what it is, regardless of how much you wish it could be changed. Unless you have discovered the magic of time travel, you might as well learn to accept your age.

Every age you pass through will have ups and downs, and you must contend with them. The early teen years are years of promise, preparation, and anticipation. There is not a great deal of independence, and others still help you make decisions. For most teens these years are a period of preparation for and a gradual easing into the adult world. Too much independence at your age often results in a period of reckless trial-and-error experimenting and no real preparation. Make no mistake, you need to prepare for life as an adult, and this process should not be taken lightly or rushed.

During the next few years, you will undergo more changes than in any other period of life. There is no need to hurry these years along. Take your time, plan, and prepare for the years that lie ahead. The independence and freedom of choice adults enjoy is something most people your age can see quite well. What is not as clearly visible are the responsibilities and potential pitfalls of the adult world.

Today is your reality. You know it's unrealistic to think that you can change your age, so my advice to you and your friends is to learn to accept life's different stages as they come and make the most of them. Once learned, this valuable lesson can be carried through life. Do not wish your life away. You will be old soon enough!

Hey, Mr. McRay,

When my friends and I get together on the weekends we let go sometimes and do some serious drinking. My girlfriend's dad has a cabin that we use. He doesn't care as long as we don't get caught or cause any damage. No one drives afterward, so we drink as much as we want. We don't do this often, but when we do, we really let our hair down. One of the girls who used to go with us says we've got a drinking problem. I don't see that. Maybe we overdo once in a while, but we don't drink all the time like alcoholics, and we don't drive while drunk. We don't even leave the cabin because some of us are under age. So what's the big problem?

—Larry

Heavy Drinking Is a Serious Problem

Dear Larry,

Have you ever heard of binge drinking? It is the periodic or sporadic consumption of large amounts of alcohol in a limited amount of time. It sounds as if you and some of your friends either are or are becoming binge drinkers. And although it may not meet the traditional profile of a classic alcoholic, binge drinking is most definitely a drinking problem and a serious concern. Several deaths, particularly on college campuses, have been attributed to binge drinking that went too far. National publicity of these deaths has contributed to a growing public awareness of the risks and dangers associated with sporadic, heavy drinking.

Drinking alcohol is socially acceptable among adults if not done excessively, but social acceptance has created a dangerous misconception about alcohol. Regardless of the beverage—whether beer, wine, mixed drinks, or wine coolers—when you drink, you are putting a powerful drug into your body. That drug is alcohol, and it most definitely has an effect. It affects judgment, perception, and various physical functions of the body. The level of that effect seems to be directly related to how much you drink over a given period of time. The more you drink in a short period of time, the greater the potential effect of the alcohol. However, regardless of the quantity or the time, it is undeniable that impairment—both physical and mental—begins with the first drink. And the ingestion of a concentration of alcohol places a heavier burden on the body to detoxify itself.

Binge drinkers often try to convince themselves that they don't have a problem just because they don't drink all the time. They're wrong. The chief concern with sporadic heavy drinking is that it's a bigger dose of the drug in a shorter time, and the resulting effects of the alcohol can be dramatic. Some people have fallen into comas or been brain damaged, conditions certainly difficult to deal with at a remote cabin.

Another disturbing result is that, among young people, even moderate drinking can start a pattern of consumption that can quickly become destructive. Numerous studies have proven beyond question that more than half of the adults who have a serious drinking problem started drinking as teenagers.

I am pleased to see that you mentioned twice in your letter than no one drives when you are drinking. I do not condone your excessive, unsupervised drinking, but at least you're not compounding your poor judgment by driving.

I'd like to close with a comment about your friend's dad, and please feel free to share it with him. If he is allowing minors to drink at his cabin, he is shamefully deficient in good judgment, and he is knowingly and willfully breaking the law.

Hey, Mr. McRay,

I'm a senior, and, like all seniors, I'm facing a lot of major decisions. My parents, teachers, counselors, and friends all have advice to offer. I know they mean well, but I get really confused at times. I don't want someone else making my decisions for me, but it's tough to know what to do. The decisions I'm facing are no longer simple choices with easy right or wrong answers. Decisions I'm about to make, like what college to go to, what field to go into, and what relationships to keep, will affect my life for a long time. When I was younger it was easier. I didn't have many big decisions to make, and things never seemed confusing. Am I the only senior who is this confused?

—Confused Senior?

Making Tough Decisions

Dear Confused Senior,

This reply should really be addressed "Dear Confused Seniors" because you're not alone. Most seniors (at least those carefully considering their future) are somewhat confused. You are right—when you were younger things were simpler. You didn't have many decisions to make, and most of the important ones were made for you. Now that you're assuming more personal responsibility, there are decisions only you can make. Some uncertainty is natural, and where there is uncertainty there is bound to be some confusion. Maturity means accepting responsibility for yourself and making tough decisions among many alternatives with little certainty.

As you mature, you will face periods of personal confusion. They are part of growing up, but you need to keep them in perspective. Don't let them overwhelm you. Get used to life's uncertainties and learn to actively deal with them. Seek advice from those you trust, consider your alternatives, decide what is best for you, and trust in your ability to make the best of your decisions.

There is an adage that says, "Uncertainty is the flagship of opportunity." Don't be afraid to set sail!

Hey, Mr. McRay,

I'm a senior in high school and have been accepted into a nursing school. I've always been interested in medicine and helping people. The problem is that I'm a guy! At first my friends made some jokes about me wanting to be a nurse. They thought I wanted to go into nursing because I would be around a lot of girls. Now that I've been accepted, they tease me all the time. Most of the time it doesn't bother me, but I don't want to be thought of as weird. Now I've started hesitating when I'm asked what I'm going to do after high school, and sometimes I say I'm not sure yet. I still have time to change my mind before fall. My grades are good, so I could go into something else if I want to.

My mother is a nurse and has always liked what she does. I guess it made a good impression on me. I know there's nothing wrong with guys wanting to be nurses, but I wish I could get my friends to get off my case because of it. Do you have any thoughts on how I might do this?

—Barry

He Wants to Be a Nurse

Dear Barry,

Congratulations! Nursing and all other fields of medicine need all the compassionate, dedicated, and interested people they can attract. Your decision is admirable, and in no way should you be swayed by some teasing from your friends. A career decision is too important to be made or changed because of some teasing. They tease you because they don't understand your decision.

Before you become too concerned about your friends' reactions to your career choice, ask yourself the following simple questions: Have you explained to your friends why you want to go into nursing? Do your friends know anything about the field of nursing and the demands nursing school will place on you? Have you told your friends that their teasing bothers you?

It's not advisable or necessary for you to share your deepest feelings on the matter, but tell your friends that your decision to go into nursing is a very serious one. Let them know that you admire your mother and her nursing work and that your decision is an informed one, not based on a whim. They may not understand how serious your decision is to you. They may also have little understanding about modern nursing. Try explaining to them, using some specific examples, why you have chosen to pursue nursing as a career.

Teasing for any reason can quickly turn cruel. Whether the teasers intend to or not, they can hurt the people they pick on and can cause some undesirable reactions. Your friends have caused you to have some doubts about your career choice. You must either try to reduce their teasing or learn to ignore it. If you take it too seriously and you alter your career plans, you would be making a serious, long-term mistake. Be proud of your decision and follow through!

Hey, Mr. McRay,

There is a swim team at the "Y" that I would like to join. The problem is that there are only fifteen spots. There are a lot more people than that who want to be on the team. Because there are so many, the two coaches said we would have to try out. I think it'll be very hard for me to make this team because there are guys who have been on the team before, and I think the coaches know some of the other parents. We just moved, so my parents do not know many people here yet. I do not even think I am going to try it because I do not think I stand much of a chance, and I do not like to fail at things. Would you try it?

—Gerrick

If You Think Negative Thoughts, You Defeat Yourself

Dear Gerrick,

With the attitude you've expressed, I'd agree there is not much reason for you even to try to make this swim team. You've defeated yourself before you have begun. Having never seen you swim, I can't evaluate your swimming ability. However, swimming is like most things in life— if you approach it with the wrong attitude, it becomes almost impossible to do your best. If you want to make this team, you will need to do your best, and that means approaching the tryouts with a positive attitude. Assuming that last year's team members have automatic spots because the coaches know their parents is no way to build a positive attitude. Instead, you have created a self-defeating attitude.

A self-defeating attitude is the result of negative thoughts about yourself and the situations in which you find yourself. Such an attitude limits your ability to do your best, but it does provide you with an excuse if you fail. You can tell yourself, "Well, I told you so. I knew you'd fail." The decision you must make is a simple one. If you want to make this team, you'll need a positive attitude to do your best, and believing that the deck is stacked against you or being afraid to fail is no way to build a positive attitude. To do your best, you must see yourself as a swimmer with the talent and ability to make the team. Approach the tryouts believing that you can and will make the team. Develop a positive view of yourself as a swimmer and member of the swim team. If, after the tryouts, you find that you have not made the team, accept that fact and move on. Failure is a risk of trying, and trying is a part of life.

Although failure is not a pleasant consequence, our failures are seldom fatal, and they usually provide opportunities to learn and grow. One of the best is the opportunity to develop perseverance, which is the ability and willingness to keep going, even in the face of failure. Don't be defeated before you start by negative thoughts!

Hey, Mr. McRay,

My school is having a semiformal holiday dance. I was asked to go and I want to a lot, but I may not be able to go because of babysitting. I babysit for two little girls in my neighborhood. I am their only sitter, and I have always been available when they need me. I spend most Saturday evenings with the girls. The dance is on a Saturday evening. They have not asked me to sit that evening, but I think they might. If they do, I don't want to let them down. If I tell them that I can't sit, they may find another sitter. If they get another sitter, they may not call me anymore. I really like being with the girls, and I don't want them to find another sitter, but I also want to go to the holiday dance. What should I do?

—Sincerely, Farrah

Five Steps for Making Decisions

Dear Farrah,

The dilemma you describe is understandable, and the commitment you feel toward the girls you babysit is admirable. However, you've made two assumptions that may or may not be accurate. You haven't yet been asked to babysit the evening of the dance—you're just assuming you will be. You may not be asked. If you aren't, there's no problem. You've also assumed that if you choose the dance over babysitting, you won't be asked to babysit again. Unless you made a long-term commitment to babysit every Saturday evening, you have every right to make other plans. You might want to tell the folks you sit for that you are planning to go out that evening, if you regularly sit on Saturday nights, but even that is just a courtesy. Just because you often sit on Saturday nights doesn't mean you're obligated to sit every Saturday evening.

Throughout your life, you will be called upon to make countless decisions. There is a simple decision-making model that will serve you well if you use it. That model has five basic steps:

1. Identify the decision that must be made.
2. Determine who will make the decision.
3. Gather information; do not depend on assumptions.
4. Consider the possible consequences.
5. Make the decision that will result in the most desirable set of consequences.

In this case, you have identified the decision that must be made. You have also determined who will make the decision, and that is you. Now you need to gather information. Call the folks you sit for and tell them what your plans are. Even if they did want you to sit—though they hadn't asked you yet—you will have to make a decision, and it seems you have already decided to go to the dance. Don't assume they'll be angry that you are unable to sit. They may change their plans, or they may say they'll find another sitter for that evening and will call you the next time they need a sitter. On the other hand, if they did expect you to sit and are angry that you're unavailable that evening—even though they hadn't asked you yet—you need to reconsider your role as their babysitter. They have no right to expect you to be available every Saturday evening unless you have explicitly agreed to this. Once you have replaced your assumptions with facts, you will be in a better position to make a decision. This is true of most decisions you will make in life.

Hey, Mr. McRay,

   Every time I think I am finally growing up, I cry about something. I thought when I got older I would outgrow crying. I get very embarrassed because crying makes me feel like a baby. I was watching a movie with my parents, and I could feel that I was going to cry. I didn't want my sisters to see me, so I left the room.

   Even though I get embarrassed when I cry, I sometimes feel better when I do. The last time I got really mad at my sister. I felt like I was going to blow up. I was so mad I started to cry, but after a while I felt better. I think this is a kind of trap. Crying can make you feel better about some things, but then you feel like a jerk because you are acting like a baby. How can you get out of this trap?

—Karl

Crying Is an Innate Reaction

Dear Karl,

There has long been a notion that only babies cry. I can understand why you might think that crying is inappropriate. This is true for all of us, but if you are a guy it can be even worse. I don't know how this idea got started, but I do know how it has been kept alive. Crying is a very natural response to certain stimuli. Crying is generally a reaction; something that makes you feel sad, scared, angry, or hurt can cause you to cry. Some people cry when they are very happy or when something they have been very concerned about is finally over. There are many emotions and feelings that make people cry.

For some reason, we have come to believe that adults don't cry and that men aren't supposed to cry even when they are boys. I don't support this line of thinking. Very few of us are going to be able to go through life without experiencing a variety of strong emotions and feelings. I for one would not want to go through life without such experiences. Coping with these emotions and feelings is something we all must learn to do. Crying is a very powerful way to deal with certain emotions, and I don't feel that anyone has the right to tell us that we can't cry if we feel like it.

I wouldn't suggest that you handle all of your problems by crying about them, but in certain situations crying is a good and natural response, and I can see no point in fighting it. The next time you feel embarrassed because you have cried about something consider this: Crying is a natural response to some emotion or feeling. So is laughing. Babies cry and babies laugh. If you are going to feel like a baby when you cry, then I guess you should feel like a baby when you laugh. There is no more reason to be ashamed of crying than there is to be ashamed of laughing.

I hope your life is filled with far more laughter than tears. But I also hope you can experience enough of life so all of your human sensitivity can be touched. If you do, you can expect to shed some tears now and then. One of the finest compliments anyone can be paid is to be called a sensitive person. Do not cheat yourself by becoming insensitive to your feelings and emotions.

Hey, Mr. McRay,

For a long time I was a chronic worrier. I worried about everything. I worried so much I would often forget what I was worrying about. I worried about my family, my friends, people I thought were my enemies, and myself. At times I think I even tried to worry *for* my family and friends. If I knew one of them was having a problem, I worried about how they would deal with it and what might happen to them. If I didn't have something to worry about, I was sure something terrible was just about to happen, so then I would have something to worry about.

I wasted much of my time in junior high and high school worrying about what did or didn't happen and what would or wouldn't happen. I know now I cheated myself out of a great deal of fun and pleasure, and I must have missed many good times because I was so busy worrying.

After high school I went to college and at first I took my worrying with me. I had a whole new environment to worry about. In fact, there was so much to worry about, I simply ran out of time. I had to start being more selective about what I worried about. There were just not enough hours in the day to cover all of my worries. When I had to start picking my worries, I knew I had a problem, and I knew I had to do something about it. I was tired of filling every day with the worries of yesterday and tomorrow. The problem was I had worried so long that I had become very good at it. I had a horrible habit I had to deal with. Maybe I had myself convinced that worrying was something people were supposed to do. I was a quiet person and a serious student, so I usually worried in silence. I seldom shared my worries with anyone else. I suppose I just thought everyone worried all of the time.

Slowly I began to realize that most of the things I worried about were absolutely pointless. At the same time, I began to understand that even if there was a problem or something to be concerned about, worrying was going to do very little to help me. All worrying was going to do was confuse the issue and make it even tougher for me either to ignore the situation or to plan and take the appropriate action. It takes rational thought, careful planning, and purposeful action to deal with a problem, and worrying is none of the above.

Soon I found myself worrying less and less. When I did worry, it was no longer an intense, lingering worry that prevented me from taking the steps needed to find a solution. Also, my worrying began to be more action-oriented. I began to think about the things I worried about in terms of what I could *do* about them. I began thinking of possible actions or reactions because I was no longer content to spend my days in a "what if" state of mind. I had been a prisoner of my worries long enough. Now I had better things to do with my time.

Today, years after I first came to terms with my unproductive habit of worrying, I still periodically find myself trapped by the worries of yesterday and tomorrow. However, I now find it increasingly easier to stop worrying and start thinking in a more positive and productive way. I have also learned to talk with those who are close to me (my husband and friends) about the things that concern me. I have stopped worrying alone.

When I started to tell this story, I had no idea I would go on this long. I just wanted to share my experience because I thought you might be able to use me as an example in one of your columns. The world that today's teens live in is a great deal more complicated than when I was a teen. By sharing my story with you, maybe you could remind your readers that worrying is usually pointless. Today's teens should know that, instead of worrying, they should think in realistic terms about the problems they face, and try to think of how they can solve or deal with the situations they face. I also want to remind all worriers that worrying in silence only makes the problems seem bigger.

—Sincerely, Brenda

Worry Is a Waste of Time

Dear Brenda,

What a story! I hope you don't mind, but I shared your story as you presented it. I could not agree with you more. Worrying is a waste of time, but it can indeed become a chronic problem. I hope anyone reading this column stops to think about the amount of time he or she spends in useless, unproductive worry. Thanks very much for sharing!

Hey, Mr. McRay,

    I am a high school senior, and I've been invited to several parties. I want to go, but I know there will be drinking and I have a problem with that. If I got caught, I'd be in all kinds of trouble, and my parents would kill me. If I go and don't drink, everyone makes fun. The last time I went to a party, there was a girl who didn't drink and they really got on her. The following week in school, someone tied a baby bottle to the antenna of her car.

    I want to be with my friends, and I want to have fun, but I don't want to get into trouble. I've had beer before, and I don't really like it. I have heard that adults who are alcoholics started to drink when they were young. Also, if I get into any trouble while driving and alcohol is involved, my parents won't let me use their car anymore. I just don't know what I should do. When my friends talk about parties, beer seems to be all that we talk about.

—Yours, Mike

To Drink or Not to Drink?

Dear Mike,

Unfortunately, too many people think the words "celebrating" and "drinking" are synonymous. I certainly can understand the peer pressure you talk about when it comes to drinking. It has been some years since I was a high school senior, but I felt pressure to drink with my friends too. It wasn't easy to deal with such peer pressure then, and I assume it's no easier now. Most of the decisions you will make in life are personal, and making personal decisions is not always easy. As your friend found out when she received a baby bottle, some decisions you feel are right will not be accepted by friends or family.

As you and your friends know, drinking under the age of 21 is illegal. It's also safe to assume that most parents do not support underage drinking. It is good to be aware of these legal and parental limitations, but your other reasons for not wanting to drink are actually more important. You won't always be under the watchful eye of your parents, and you're surely aware of times and places where you can drink and not get caught. If these are the only reasons you avoid drinking, you may find it very difficult to resist even slight peer pressure to do so. Both of these reasons are *external* reasons, limitations placed on your behavior by laws and your parents. However, if you have resolved to avoid underage drinking, that becomes an *internal* reason, a limitation that you determined for yourself. Armed with such an internal or personal resolve to avoid illegal alcohol, you will find it much easier to stick with your decision, regardless of the pressure exerted by your friends.

I don't know enough about alcoholism to tell you about the correlation between early drinking and alcoholism, but I believe there is some truth to this assumption. I do know a lot, however, about driving, and I can assure you that when you've been drinking, your driving ability is definitely impaired. In fact, drinking is one of the chief factors in fatal automobile accidents.

The ultimate decision is yours alone. I think you have a good foundation to make a wise personal decision about drinking.

Hey, Mr. McRay,

There are times when I really feel good about myself and other times when I don't. Sometimes I think it's my faul and other times it's not. I know everyone goes through times when they don't feel good about themselves, and I know I'll have times like that. I guess no one is up all the time. I would just like to understand more about what makes me feel like this. I'd also like to have more control over how I feel. I don't think it's right for people to make you feel bad about yourself.

—Yours, Blake

Self-Esteem Is Very Complex

Dear Blake,

From time to time we all experience ups and downs, and I would guess that we have all wondered what causes them. There are many explanations, and as you already know, these periodic changes are normal. However, when you develop such a poor view of yourself that it prevents you from being the person you want to be, there is a problem.

For our purposes, let's use the term "self-esteem" to refer to the picture you have of yourself. Your self-esteem is based on a number of considerations, feelings, and impressions. It can be affected by daily circumstances, other people, and especially you. Your self-esteem is a very complex part of you that can and does change. Some of your self-esteem changes will be major while others will be minor. Some changes will have a long-term impact while others will not. For example, suppose you say or do something that embarrasses you. You may not be pleased with yourself at that time, but such an incident will probably not cause major or long-term changes in the view you have of yourself. On the other hand, you may enter into a personal or professional relationship that causes the view you have of yourself and others to change. That may not have an immediate effect, but it may be a long-term effect.

Normal ups and downs are generally not difficult to deal with. However, sometimes these ups and downs go beyond the normal range. Understanding a little about self-esteem it can make it much easier to prevent these big changes and to deal with them when they do arise.

As individuals we are each unique. This is part of what makes life so interesting, and it's important that we understand and respect the uniqueness of others. By so doing, we allow them to be the people they wish to be and to do the things they feel they must and should do. In the same way, we must demand for ourselves the right to be the persons we want to be and to do the things we feel we must do. (I offer this piece of advice assuming that you understand there are moral, safety, ethical, and legal limitations on your ability and freedom to "be yourself.")

As you go through periodic self-esteem changes, consider the following:

1. Respect the right of others to be themselves, and it will be easier for them to respect your right.
2. Take a good look at yourself from time to time. Others may see something in you that you are missing. Even though you are the principal artist of the picture you have of yourself, it won't hurt to consider the thoughts and opinions of others.
3. Look for the good in others. It will help you to see the good in yourself.
4. Let go of failures, setbacks, and mistakes. Learn from them, but be willing to forgive yourself, so that you can move on.
5. Keep your view of yourself in perspective; no one is all good or all bad. Paint your self-portrait on a broad canvas, considering the whole person.

Some simple advice from former First Lady Eleanor Roosevelt may provide the best possible summary to this column: "No one can make you feel inferior without your consent!"

PARENTS AND SIBLINGS

A Broken Trust Takes Time to Heal
She Feels Weird for Getting Along with Her Parents
Explain Your Feelings to Your Parents
Daughter Is Worried about Mom
Brother's Privileges Leave Sister Feeling Cheated
Siblings Often Feel Neglected in Larger Families
You Don't Have to Be Like Your Brother
Kids Are Not to Blame for Divorce
Splits Are Not Always Permanent
On Being a Role Model
Teens Offer Differing Views on Adoption
Father's Unemployment Disrupts Entire Family

Hey, Mr. McRay,

I told my parents a lie, which I know is wrong, but my parents are punishing me for it a lot more that I think they should. They are really making a big deal out of this. It's like I never told them the truth once in my life. I told them I was going to a dance at the school, and they found out some of us went to a mall near the school. My aunt saw me, and she told my parents She wasn't trying to get me in trouble; she just told them she saw me. When they asked me where I was, I said I was at the school the whole time. So now it's a big deal. I feel like they'll never trust me again. Of course I'm grounded, but what's worse is that now they check on everything I say and they remind me all the time that I lied to them. This is hurting our relationship, and I think they should back off and get over it.

—Carmen

A Broken Trust Takes Time to Heal

Dear Carmen,

Don't brush off what has happened to you and your parents. I disagree that it's not a big deal. Lying *is* a big deal. You break a trust when you lie to someone; it takes time to regain that trust. This is particularly true between children and their parents. The parent-child relationship is a complex one combining many emotions. At the core of these emotions is a mutual trust. I doubt seriously if your parents will *never* trust you again, but it will take some time for them to rebuild their trust. Let me explain.

Prior to this incident, the relationship between you and your parents probably had a high level of trust, which is indicated by their reaction to your lie. If you told them something, they could be confident that you had told them the truth, based on the long sequence of times you had been truthful. Their confidence in you and what you said provided a level of security they appreciated. Your lie has destroyed their confidence in your word. If you're lying, they figure, you might be engaging in more dangerous behavior. As a result they feel far less secure about your safety and well-being than they did before, and they feel they must watch you more closely.

The level of trust that existed between you and your parents has been damaged, but it's not totally destroyed. You will have to work to rebuild their confidence in your ability and willingness to tell the truth. By so doing, you will reestablish the level of security they had felt before. I am not going to ask you why you chose to lie to your parents. That's a question you must answer yourself. But you now can see how a single lie can alter the level of trust in a relationship. You've created an unfortunate situation for yourself, but you can learn a great deal from it.

The first step toward resolving this problem is being forthright with your parents. Tell them why you lied. Don't offer excuses, only an explanation. If you understand why your lie caused them such concern, say so. If you don't fully understand, discuss it with them. Let them explain why your lie makes them worry about you now, when they didn't before. Explain that their trust is important to you, that you want to have it back. Assure them that this was an isolated incident, which you regret, and that you want to prove to them that you are trustworthy. Ask specifically what they want to see in you that would show them you are sincere. Then make good on your word. If handled properly, this incident can actually strengthen your relationship with your parents because you all now have an appreciation for the importance of mutual trust and how you feel when it has been shaken.

Hey, Mr. McRay,

Most of my friends have problems with their parents. They're always talking about how they fight and how they can hardly wait to get out of their house. One of my friends even said in class she wants to go to college just to get away from her parents.

I don't have any big problems with my parents. We get along great, and I think we are a real good family. We sometimes get angry, but it's not a big thing that goes on all the time. We love each other, and we're not afraid to say it. Because of the way most of my friends have it, I'm afraid to say too much about my family. I don't want my friends to think I'm weird, but I don't want them to think my family is like theirs either. Am I really strange?

—Sincerely, Gayle

She Feels Weird for Getting Along with Her Parents

Dear Gayle,

A good family is one of the richest blessings you can have! A good family is nothing to apologize for, nor is it anything you should be ashamed of. However, it can be difficult to talk about a happy family in the midst of people who do not have the type of family you have. I can easily understand the pressure you are feeling. I have felt some of that same pressure at different points in my life. Sometimes I'm tempted to overreact when I hear people say things like, "There's something wrong with the kids nowadays!" or "All kids hate their parents during their teen years!" These are generalizations that some people accept as being true of most families.

No family is perfect! All families have to deal with problems and difficult situations. However, family members who are bound by love, mutual respect, and commitment have learned to deal with their problems. They stick together; they identify their problems; and together they work toward solutions.

There has been a great deal of talk recently about the destruction of the American family. It is certainly true that the once "typical" family is hardly typical anymore. However, it is equally true that the family is still the very backbone of American society and the foundation for our way of life. It is true that many families are unable to fulfill basic human needs. These needs can generally be classified as emotional, social, or physical needs. Such families are often termed "dysfunctional."

Dysfunctional families are a problem. There are a number of factors that contribute to the development of dysfunctional families. These factors range from drug and alcohol abuse to hard economic times. Regardless of the causes, some of your friends live in troubled and dysfunctional families. You might try to help those friends, offering them some of the care and understanding they need. However, one thing that will not help them at all is pretending that you also live in a dysfunctional family. Although it would not be wise to boast, having a happy, loving family is nothing to feel weird about.

If you are in a position to do so, share your family with some of your friends. Give them the opportunity to spend time with your family. You need not make any judgments of your family or theirs. Just let them share some time. They may see that all families are not dysfunctional, and they may develop a more positive view of what their family life could be with a little effort.

Hey, Mr. McRay,

My parents always blame me if there is something wrong at my house. I am the oldest. My younger brother and sister never get blamed for anything. Everything is always my fault. I even got screamed at one time for something that happened in the family room when I was already in bed.

I have talked to my parents, but they just say it's my imagination. One time my dad said I should always be setting an example for the younger kids. I guess I should, but everything is not always my fault. Sometimes I get really mad at my younger brother and sister because they keep getting away with things. They think they get screamed at all the time, and they think I get away with things because I am the oldest.

I know I shouldn't get mad at them, but how can I make my parents understand?

—Signed, Becky

Explain Your Feelings to Your Parents

Dear Becky,

In any family, there are bound to be times when you will be blamed for things that you did not do or are not responsible for. This is not only true in families, but it is true of almost everything in life. When this happens, it is essential that you consider the circumstances carefully then react in a way that will clarify your role in a particular situation. It is unwise to accept blame for things which you are not responsible, but it is just as unwise to overreact or react negatively.

Whether you are being singled out more than your siblings or not, if you think you are, you should do something about it. Don't be hasty or rude—that won't accomplish a thing. Begin by telling your parents how you feel. Instead of telling them that they are picking on you and accusing them of treating you differently than your brother and sister, tell them that this is what it feels like to you. In this way you are not accusing them. You are just sharing your feelings. When you talk with your parents, try to have some specific examples to share with them. Remember that anger, rudeness, and accusations rarely solve problems.

After you've had a chance to talk with your parents, listen to their response. If they tell you they expect more of you because you should be a role model for the younger children in the family, you might reply that you want to be a good model, but that it hurts when you're blamed for things that you didn't do. By explaining your feelings to your parents, you will be helping them become more sensitive to you. Sharing your feelings may help them to keep their expectations of you in perspective. If you're not being picked on, as you believe you are, your parents will have an opportunity to show you this. In either case, you will be moving closer to solving your problem.

Hey, Mr. McRay,

Do you think members of a family should share things? I do and I think my parents are not telling me something. I think my mother is sick, but my parents are not saying anything to me. She went to the doctor's just for a checkup, and then she had to go back two other times. Between those appointments, she went to the hospital for a morning. They said she was getting a test. When they came home from the doctor's the last time, they both looked worried. They tried to act like everything was okay, but I just know something is wrong. All they said was that my mother was going to the hospital and that my grandmother was coming to stay with us.

I have tried to ask them what is going on, but they just say something like "It's nothing" or "Everything is going to be fine." I am real worried. I do not know what to do. Can you help me?

—Sincerely, Denni

Daughter Is Worried about Mom

Dear Denni,

One of life's greatest fears is the fear of the unknown! Your worries are a result of your fears of the unknown. When you face an unknown situation, there are three ways you can react. You can view the situation positively and be an optimist; you can view it negatively and be a pessimist; or you can ignore it and be simply unconcerned. No one is always an optimist, always a pessimist, or always unconcerned. Instead, people tend to act differently, depending on what kind of situation they face and their relationship to it. Unfortunately, unknown situations that are closest to us are often the easiest ones to be pessimistic about. I think this may be true in your case. You don't know what your mother's situation is; you're thinking negatively about it; and your negative thinking has produced a great deal of fear.

Your parents may not be sharing more with you in this instance because they may assume you know more than you actually do. Or your mother may have a serious medical problem, and they feel it would be difficult for you to understand. On the other hand, your mother may be dealing with something minor and manageable, and your parents see no reason to discuss it with you. And your parents may be saying very little because they just want to keep this matter private while they deal with their own feelings about it.

Even in the closest families, individuals have the right to some degree of personal privacy. Though you feel a need to know more, you must balance that need with some sensitivity. If your parents want to keep this matter to themselves for a time, you must be sensitive to their wishes. However, your parents must also be sensitive to your needs and fears.

I suggest you begin by talking with your father. Explain your concerns, and be honest about your fears. My guess is that he will respond by sharing and helping you deal realistically with this situation. He may not be able to end your fears, but you will at least have a better view of the situation, and if there is reason for concern, your concern will be realistic. Regardless of what you learn about your mom's coming hospital stay, fear is a basically useless emotion. Fear will not help you support your mother or your father.

Hey, Mr. McRay,

My brother is three years younger than I am. I'm 17 and in 12th grade. He is just 14 and is in 9th grade. I don't think my parents treat us fairly. I was not allowed to date until I was 16, and my parents were strict about this. My brother has been allowed to date, and he is not even 15.

Another thing is curfew. When I was 14, I had to be in on weekends at 11 p.m. I was not allowed out on school nights after 9 p.m. My brother stays at the mall as late as he wants. We both are allowed out until midnight on weekends if our parents know where we are. I do not think this is fair because I am older. He is getting to do a lot more at a younger age than I ever did. I think that if he gets into trouble, things could change for both of us. I feel like I have been cheated because I had to wait longer to get to do certain things and stay out later than 11 p.m. Do you think this is very fair?

—Yours, Pam

Brother's Privileges Leave Sister Feeling Cheated

Dear Pam,

Since your brother has some privileges that you didn't have at his age, it's easy to see why you might feel that you were treated unfairly. However, "fair" is a relative term. There are many conditions and circumstances that affect the guidelines parents set for their children. A major task all parents face is determining if and when their children are individually ready for various freedoms, responsibilities, and privileges.

Parents grow along with their children. Parents are not the same throughout the developmental years of their children. They change as they learn more about themselves and their children. These changes are generally in the direction of feeling more and more comfortable allowing children to assume greater responsibility for themselves. As children do this, they have much more freedom to do as they please. As they learn to handle this increased freedom responsibly, parents usually tend to grant more. As you can see, this is a cycle where a demonstrated ability to assume responsibility results in opportunities to assume even more.

In families with more than one child, the oldest child begins this cycle. Parents usually get more comfortable, allowing younger brothers and sisters to start the process at an earlier age, and this is not only because of individual differences in the children. Instead, it is more the result of the parents' ability to deal with changes teens go through. Once an older brother or sister has "broken the ice," parents are often better prepared to deal with the changes when younger children come along. Yes, children of the same family may enjoy different levels of personal freedom. What seems to be unfair may actually be the result of larger circumstances. Be careful when making comparison judgments because you may be comparing things that are quite different.

Hey, Mr. McRay,

There are seven children in my family. It's great to have a big family with lots of brothers and sisters, but there's one problem. I feel like I get ignored by my parents. I am the second from the youngest, and I think that my parents don't have time for me. I haven't said this to them because it might hurt their feelings. I haven't said anything to my brothers or sisters either because they might think I'm mad at them. My oldest brother is married, and I go to his house whenever I am allowed. He always has time for me and so does his wife.

Do you think I should say anything to my parents? If I should say something to them, what do you think I should tell them?

—Yours, Allison

Siblings Often Feel Neglected in Larger Families

Dear Allison,

Regardless of the number of children in a family, there is always a need for parents and children to spend time together. For most parents, making time for their children is both important and pleasurable. However, there aren't endless hours in each day. When you take time out for work schedules, social commitments, and basics like sleeping and eating, often there's not much time left. In a family of seven children, the time that's left could be difficult to divide.

Unless your parents schedule specific times to spend with you and your brothers and sisters, there may be times when you feel as though you're not getting any of their attention. When this happens, it's not because your parents are purposely ignoring you. You may also feel you're not getting any of their attention when your brothers and sisters are going through a special time in life. For example, when your brother got married, I imagine he was the center of attention from all of you. As your sisters graduate from high school, they will be getting a great deal of attention from your parents. Again, they are not purposely ignoring you. I would guess that if you talked with your brothers and sisters, they might tell you they've had similar feelings—perhaps they still have them. In all families this happens sometimes, and in big families it's likely to happen more often.

Tell your parents how you feel. When you do, try not to accuse them of ignoring you, and try not to make them feel guilty. Instead, explain that you know they're busy, but that you would like to spend more time with them. Be prepared with some suggestions of things you'd like to do. For example, if you have a favorite hobby or a school activity that you enjoy, ask your parents to help you. Invite them to take an active part. Ask them if there's something they're involved in that could include you. Maybe your mother is a member of a club or social organization that has activities in which you too could get involved.

Frequently children try to draw away from their parents as they get older. I enjoy reading a letter from a teen who wants to spend more time with her parents. Share your feelings with your mom and dad. I think they will be very pleased and will make every effort to spend more time with you. Even though spending time with their children is something most parents really enjoy, they often have to be reminded to do more of it!

Hey, Mr. McRay,

My brother and I hardly ever get along. I try to be nice to him, but usually it just doesn't work. My brother is 16 and I am 15. There are times he makes me feel I shouldn't be around. My brother is in sports and in "Who's Who Among American High School Students." As I come along, teachers and other people at school want me to be like my brother. I don't want to be like someone else. I like to be myself. I do the best I can, and I feel that is not good enough. My brother and I always seem to fight about that. When I do something wrong, lots of times he'll punch me. Other times, if I do something righ,t he claps sarcastically as if I just learned to do it. When he calls me names and tells me that life would be a lot better if I wasn't on this earth, I feel like I'm not wanted. Should I feel guilty? Please help!

—Yours truly, Angela

You Don't Have to Be Like Your Brother

Dear Angela,

As long as there have been brothers and sisters, there have been squabbling, teasing, name-calling, and some periodic slaps and bumps. However, in your case, the slaps and bumps have become punches; the name-calling has become hurtful; and the teasing has affected your feelings about yourself.

Relationships between brothers and sisters are very individual. Sometimes the ages and sex of the siblings matter, and sometimes they don't. It can be very close in some aspects and very distant in others, even between the same pair of siblings. Because you share so much and have so much in common, it can be difficult to establish your own identity. Often in a family one of the children will dominate. This might happen because one child is more successful and receives more of the family's attention. A child may also dominate in less desirable ways, such as frequent use of insensitive comments, ongoing teasing designed to hurt, or unwanted punching or slapping. Regardless of the reason(s), when one child is permitted to dominate, the others suffer.

Your brother's successes are wonderful for him. He has every reason to be proud of himself, and you should applaud his successes. However, no one has the right to place you in his shadow. You are an individual, with the right to make your own way in life, the will to seek out and follow your own desires, the ability to develop your own skills and talents, and the freedom to address your own failures and successes. I can think of nothing worse than being sentenced to spend a lifetime walking in someone else's shadow or following in someone else's footsteps.

Though your brother may not be trying to hurt or belittle you with his comments and his actions, you seem to be taking him seriously. Let him know that the things he says and does hurt you and that you'd like him to stop. You also need to develop a more positive view of yourself. Don't look at yourself to see how well you can compete with your brother, or anyone else for that matter. Instead, look at yourself to find your own potential, work toward goals that you set, and involve yourself in activities in which you are interested. When you feel as though people are trying to force you to become a copy of your brother, ignore them or remind them that you are not your brother—you are an individual with feelings and goals of your own.

Since the problems between you and your brother seem to stem from unfair comparisons of you to him, avoiding or ignoring such comparisons may well reduce the friction you feel. When that friction is reduced, you'll more clearly see that you are indeed wanted, that you are truly a valuable person, and that the last feeling you should have is guilt.

Hey, Mr. McRay,

My parents are getting a divorce, and my brother and I are scared. We don't know who we're going to live with yet. My brother and I want to stay together, and we don't want to have to choose between living with our mother or our father. We love them both, and we don't want to do anything to make them stop loving us. We don't know why they're getting a divorce, and we hope it's not because of us. We want to help them, but we don't know what we can do. We want them to know that we love them.

Do you have any suggestions?

—Signed, Karen

Kids Are Not to Blame for Divorce

Dear Karen,

Before I tell you anything else about divorce, let me assure you that your parents are NOT getting a divorce because of anything you or your brother did. Your parents are getting a divorce because there are problems in their relationship. For some reason or reasons, your parents are unable to work out their problems, and they have chosen to end their marriage. You should not and cannot blame yourselves for that. Also, you and your brother should not worry about being split up. When a divorce is granted, everything possible is done to keep brothers and sisters together.

In the United States there is a divorce every 30 seconds. This fact is sad but true. Even though the number of divorces has increased in recent years, dealing with the pain they can cause has not become any easier. It would be nice if every couple who marries could live happily ever after, but that simply does not happen.

Remember that even though your parents are getting a divorce, your mother is still your mother and your father is still your father. My guess is that they love you and your brother, and they won't stop loving you because of their divorce. Your parents are having a problem, and they have chosen a solution that they need to work through. A divorce will not be easy on either of your parents. They will need your love, support, and understanding. You will all be making changes, and you need to support each other. That is really the best suggestion I can offer.

You need to be open and honest with your mother and father. Don't be afraid to tell them how you are feeling. Discuss your worries and fears with them. There will be some big changes in your life, and it's only natural that you and your brother are a little scared. You and your brother should not confuse your parents' feelings for each other with their feelings for you. If you blame yourselves for the problems between your parents, you're taking responsibility for something that is not your fault.

Hey, Mr. McRay,

Some time ago I read a letter from a reader named Karen and your reply. Karen's parents were in the midst of a divorce. She and her brother were concerned that the divorce might be partly their fault. She also was worried that they would be split up. Reading her letter and your reply brought back many memories of a similar ordeal my family went through. I would like to share some of these memories with you.

My husband and I had been married 16 years, and we had three children. Things had not been going well for about a year. All we did was fight, and our family life was a wreck. Finally, my husband and I agreed to separate. We agreed that the children would stay together with me and that he could see them as often as he wanted.

At first there was some peace, but soon we all had difficulty adjusting to the separation and a pending divorce. The children grew more confused daily, and because they spent most of their time with me, I became the target of their anger and frustrations. They no longer knew what their relationship was with their father, so their time with him was frequently unpleasant as well. After some months passed, we all began to adjust a little better. We even tried a weekend together. At first it was awkward for everyone. No one really knew what to say or do, but my husband and I did discover that we both loved the children. As you said in your reply to Karen, regardless of our problems, we were still their parents and we still loved them—that hadn't changed. My husband and I also knew that splitting the kids up would never be the right thing to do.

Following that weekend together, it was clear to my husband and me that separation had not solved our problems; it simply put them aside. To solve our problems we had to face them, not run from them. Our children made us see that. We agreed to seek counseling, and, after two years, we are still together as a family. We still have some problems, but at least now we deal with them.

In your reply to Karen you said that she should not confuse her parents' feelings for each other with their feelings for her and her brother. No truer words have ever been spoken! I wish every child involved in a divorce could know this. In our case, it was the love that my husband and I had for our children that caused us to work at our relationship.

Your reply to Karen mentioned that there is a divorce every 30 seconds in the United States. Although I don't know the exact number or percent, our marriage counselor told us that there has been a dramatic increase in the number of couples getting back together after a divorce or separation. I hope this is the case for Karen's parents.

—Signed,
A Loving Wife & Mother

Splits Are Not Always Permanent

Dear Loving Wife & Mother,

Hope you don't mind, but I thought our readers should have the opportunity to read your letter. You and your family are living proof that where there is love, there is hope. Thanks for sharing.

Hey, Mr. McRay,

My stepbrother is five years younger than me. We have been living together since my mother married his father last year. We all get along OK, but when I do even the littlest thing, like leave some clothes on the floor in my room, someone tells me I'm not setting a good example. Both my mother and my stepfather tell me that Zack looks up to me, so I have to set a good example for him. I guess they're right, but it puts some real pressure on me. I always feel like I'm being watched and everything I do is judged if it's a good example for Zack. I'm glad Zack likes me. I just wish our parents did not expect me to be a perfect example for him.

—Wayne

On Being a Role Model

Dear Wayne,

When two families come together to form a new family, there is an adjustment period. It takes time for all of the people involved to become comfortable with their roles in the new family. It also takes time for each person to develop a relationship with the other members of the family. Some of what you are experiencing is part of normal adjustment. However, if you feel that you're constantly being watched and that your every move is judged for the example it sets for Zack, there is a problem.

Your first step should be to discuss your feelings with your parents. Notice I said "parents" not "parent." Discussing your feelings and concerns with your mother alone might create some additional problems. What you are experiencing is a family problem, and you need to be open about it. In this case, that means that your stepfather must be involved. If not, he may feel that you don't trust him or that he won't be sensitive to your needs.

Feeling as though you are constantly under a microscope is enough to make anyone uncomfortable. If you are frequently being told you're not setting a good example, your self-esteem will eventually begin to suffer as well. You'll lose sight of yourself as a person, and you'll only see yourself as an example for Zack. This is not good for you or Zack. Though you may not be aware of it, Zack may also be feeling some pressure. Since your parents are frequently reminding you to set a good example, my guess is that they are frequently telling Zack that he needs to follow a good example.

One of the responsibilities you have to yourself is to maintain your own identity and personality. No group to which you belong—including a family—should rob you of your identity. In fact, being a part of a family or other group should cause your personality to develop and flourish. With some additional understanding from your parents, you can be the person you really are, and at the same time be a good role model for Zack. Explain to your parents how this situation makes you feel. I'm sure it's important to your parents that you and Zack share a good relationship. Be patient, though, because it may take some time for you to notice a change.

Hey, Mr. McRay,

I am 16 and I've known for some time that I was adopted a week after I was born. I've always known, so I guess my parents told me as soon as they thought I could understand. I am very close to my parents, and we love each other very much. They told me that my natural mother was only 13 years old, and she moved away right after I was born. She has never tried to contact us, and my parents don't know anything about her. Even when I was born, they didn't know anything about my father.

A friend of mind was also adopted when she was born. All she ever talks about is finding her natural parents. She keeps telling me that there is something wrong with me because I'm not interested in finding out who my real parents are. It makes me angry when she calls them "real" parents because it's like the parents we have always lived with are not real. I told her it's no big deal to me. I love my parents who adopted me, and, no matter whom I meet, they will always be my mother and father.

I'm not going to ask you which one of us is right because I know neither of us is right. I would just like to know why some adopted children are very interested in finding their natural parents and other adopted children are not. I guess I have also thought about what would happen if I ever did meet my natural parents. Do you think it would affect how my adopted parents and I feel about each other?

—Yours, Gretchen

Teens Offer Differing Views on Adoption

Dear Gretchen,

Not seeking your natural parents is right for you while searching for her natural parents is right for your friend. There is no clear reason or set of reasons why you and your friend do not share this desire. If we looked at a large number of adopted children, I'm sure we would find many who do want to learn more about their natural parents and many who have no such interest.

Without knowing a great deal more about your friend, it is impossible to even guess why she has such a strong desire to find her natural parents. And it's more difficult to explain why she suggests there's something wrong with you because you don't share her interest. I suggest you keep in touch with your own feelings instead of reacting to or worrying about your friend's feelings.

From the sound of your letter, I think you needn't worry about any unpleasant changes in the relationship between you and your parents if you should meet either or both of your natural parents. The relationship between natural parents and their children should be a beautiful bond that provides love, motivation, security, self-esteem, and a sense of identity for a lifetime. The relationship between adoptive parents and their children should also be a beautiful bond that provides love, motivation, security, self-esteem, and a sense of identity for a lifetime. In either case, the relationship is exactly what those involved choose to make of it—nothing more and nothing less.

You and your adoptive parents have developed a loving relationship in which you feel secure, and it's not likely to be threatened as you develop other relationships and friendships. The love and security you have found with your parents are great. Don't worry about losing that relationship; just be grateful for what you have and enjoy it!

Hey, Mr. McRay:

   My dad lost his job about three months ago. At first it was not a big problem, but now it is becoming one. Around the house it gets rough at times. He is not the same guy he was before. My mother seems real depressed, even though she is doing well at her job. They argue more than they ever did before. Last week he shoved her against the wall and left the house in a rage. It really scared my sister and me. We'd like to help, but we have no idea of what to do because when we suggest anything he says he can take care of himself. What can we do?

—Seth

Father's Unemployment Disrupts Entire Family

Dear Seth,

It is important that you, your mother, and your sister try to understand what has happened to your father. You might say you know what has happened to him—he's lost his job. On the surface you would be correct, but there is much more to it than that. With the loss of his job, your dad also lost his ability to support his family, which is a hard thing to accept for a man who's been the breadwinner. He probably feels he has let you all down, even though the loss of his job may not have been his fault. Since he is failing to support you financially he may feel he is failing as a man. The fact that your mother is able to provide for the family may actually be making things worse for your dad. Even though your mother is not doing so on purpose, she could be contributing to your dad's frustration since she is now doing by herself what they once did together. If this is the case, he has a diminished sense of personal worth.

Regardless of the job or profession, the work we do is a major part of our personal identity. When people are separated from their jobs, even if it happens voluntarily, as in retirement, there is a sense of lost identity. That sense of loss is exaggerated when the separation is unexpected, involuntary, or deemed to be unjustified by the person being separated. Frustration, anger, and a feeling of hopelessness are natural responses when you are the person being separated. Your dad may be feeling some or all of these emotions, which makes him very short-tempered and unpredictable.

Most employers, particularly larger ones, provide counseling, job relocation opportunities, and career retraining courses for employees who lose their jobs. Folks who cannot find such opportunities through their employers can often find similar services through local and state unemployment and social service agencies. However, before they can benefit from these services, they have to know that they exist, and they have to be willing to take advantage of them. This is where you, your sister, and your mother can help.

In your dad's frustration, he may have overlooked services available to him. And as you said in your letter, he believes that he can take care of himself. Gently suggest he look into the services available to him, but don't make it seem as though you are ganging up on him. Be sensitive to the fact he has lost more than his job and the changes that he has gone through. Be sure to tell him you support him and respect him and that you regard his unemployment as only a temporary situation. Your interest and support will encourage your dad's efforts and will help to maintain his dignity through this difficult situation.

While you are trying to be sympathetic to your dad's situation, you have to be equally concerned for the well-being of your family. If your dad refuses to help himself or to respond to your efforts to help him, he must accept the consequences of his rage and aggressiveness toward his family. If your dad is becoming physically aggressive, he is at or very near that point. For example, shoving or perhaps striking your mother and leaving the house in a rage are intolerable. If that continues, it might be time to speak with your guidance counselor or someone from your church leadership. Your dad may need help that your family.alone is not able to provide. Seeking help will serve the best interests of your family.

WORK AND HEALTH

Hey, Mr. McRay,

Last year I got sick and didn't get better for several weeks. The doctor sent me to the hospital for some tests. They found I have diabetes. I guess you know what diabetes is, but I didn't and I was scared. At first I thought I was going to die. Then I thought that even if I did live, I wouldn't be able to do anything, and I would be at the doctor's all the time. My parents were scared too. They must have asked me how I felt a hundred times a day. Now, a year later, things are much better for me.

I wanted to tell other kids who might just be finding out about having diabetes that there are all kinds of diabetes. Some are much worse than others. I know many diabetics have to give themselves shots every day, which takes more getting used to. I only have to take a pill, monitor my blood sugar, and watch what I eat. I can eat most things. There are just some things I can't eat a lot of, like candy and ice cream. It's not ever going to go away, and I know I can't ignore it, but I have learned to live with it.

A year ago the doctor said I shouldn't worry about dying. He said if I took care of myself I could have a long and healthy life, because there is nothing else wrong with me. He also said I could do almost anything I wanted. Still, I had to learn it for myself before I could believe it. I'm happy to say he was right.

When I first found out I had diabetes I felt like I had to tell everyone. I'm not sure why, but I thought my friends had to know. At first they had all kinds of questions like about how I got it. They treated me different, too, like they were pitying or babying me. One girl in my math class even offered to do my homework for me. Now I'm just one of the crowd again, and that's what I want.

Before I got sick, I was not into any sports. Now I play tennis at school and swim at the YMCA three days each week. I'm trying to get on the Y's competitive swim team. I guess I had to prove to myself that I could do anything I wanted, and so far I can. I do more now than before, and I really enjoy tennis and swimming. This may sound strange, but finding out that I had diabetes caused me to get into things that I would never have tried.

I don't like having diabetes, but I guess I could have things that are much worse. Maybe you could tell other kids who get diabetes that it is something they can live with if they have a good attitude. Maybe they can learn from me.

—Signed, Reggie

When storm clouds appear on your horizon, do not panic. Most of them will dissipate before they reach you, and many others will have silver linings.

Teen's Positive Attitude Conquers Fear

Dear Reggie,

Your story is one about conquering fear, dealing with worries, and making the most of life. I cannot think of anyone who would not benefit from hearing your story. Thanks for sharing! Continue enjoying life, and good luck on the swim team. I'm sure you'll make it!

Hey, Mr. McRay,

I am 16 years old, and I think I'm pregnant. I don't know what to do. My parents will go crazy, and I know my boyfriend will drop me. If people find out I'm pregnant, I know they'll think horrible things about me. I'm afraid to tell anyone because then it will just get spread around. I know this is all my fault, but I'm scared and I don't know what to do. Where can I get some help?

—Signed, Dee Ann

Pregnancy Need Not Be Faced Alone

Dear Dee Ann,

Although being pregnant at your age is not something I would wish for you, it is not the end of the world. There will be difficulties and possible social and emotional adjustments. But there are people who can and will help you through this period of your life. First, you need to tell your parents and seek their support. Although their initial reactions may be anger and frustration, these will not be their lasting sentiments. You will need to give your parents time to adjust. An unplanned pregnancy always brings with it a host of changes. Even though these may be unplanned, they can be handled if those involved are patient and willing to adapt.

If your parents refuse to help you, you may find it necessary to turn to local agencies and organizations that offer free counseling and testing. Most groups that want to help young pregnant teens are staffed by caring, concerned individuals. To find these agencies, look in your telephone directory in the special "Human Services" section under "Pregnancy Concerns."

If you are pregnant, it is essential that you understand that this is not "all [your] fault," as you said in your letter. There is a shared responsibility associated with every pregnancy. If you feel your boyfriend will drop you if you are pregnant, you need to give your relationship some very serious consideration. If you question his concern for you in a crisis or his willingness to assume his rightful responsibility in a problem situation, your relationship is tragically weak.

Your statement that people will "think horrible things" about you is unfortunately true. There will be comments made that are neither kind nor charitable. You have no control over what people think or say, but you do have control over how you respond to such comments and how you let them affect you. If you choose to let them get you down, be prepared to feel down for a while. If you choose to respond by defending yourself, making excuses, or getting angry, start now getting your responses ready. I'd suggest you spend your time more productively. Strive to ignore comments meant to hurt you or put you down. Don't waste time defending yourself or making excuses. What's done is done, and you must make the best of the situation. Accepting that some situations simply are as they are is the best first step toward dealing successfully with them. It's likely that your family members have strong feelings about your pregnancy, but it's important that you not fight about it. Use the energy to map out a plan for the future. Don't make any quick decisions about your pregnancy. After seeking help, take time to consider all your options as well as the baby's.

Hey, Mr. McRay,

The last time I went to the dentist, he said I might need braces. My parents took me to another type of dentist, and he said I do. My parents are making me get them. I don't want them. I'll be getting them on just before school starts. Starting middle school is bad enough, but now I'll get teased because of the braces. I don't think I need them. They will be a bother and a waste of money. Don't you think I should decide if I get them or not?

—Yours truly, Michael

Braces Are Only a Temporary Inconvenience

Dear Michael,

Since you are beginning middle school, I will assume you are between 11 and 13. At that age, you are not prepared to make a decision about something as important as braces on your own. Decisions about braces are not simple. Your family dentist did not even attempt to make a decision. Instead, he sent you to another dentist, probably an orthodontist (a dental specialist who works with braces). And then a decision was made only after a careful examination and a conference with your parents.

Even though braces may seem like "a bother and a waste of money," they will undoubtedly result in some important long-term benefits. You may take a little teasing at first, but nowadays, more and more teenagers are getting braces—I doubt you'll be the only student at your school with them. Ignore the teasers or just laugh off their comments. You needn't pay any attention to them, and they'll probably stop when the novelty has worn off.

For the efforts of your orthodontist to be successful, you will need to work with him or her. Cooperate and you'll make the whole process more pleasant. When you think about your braces, remind yourself of this old saying: "Permanent improvement often requires some temporary inconvenience!"

Hey, Mr. McRay,

I really envy people who can express themselves and say whatever is on their minds. I feel shy, and though I talk a lot with one friend alone, if I'm in a group, I clam up. I guess I feel like I should not get into the conversation. When I do get involved, I sometimes say things I do not mean. I guess I just say things so that I will be a part of the group. What can I do to stop feeling so shy, and how can I make sure that I just say things that I mean?

—Sincerely, Sherry

Overcoming Shyness

Dear Sherry,

One of the advantages of having friends is having someone to talk to. For some people talking to friends and in front of groups comes very easily. To others, it's not so easy. From the sound of your letter, it's not easy for you. This is common and is nothing to be ashamed of.

Many people, including well-known celebrities, movie and TV stars, and government and business leaders, have difficulty talking in front of people. You'd be shocked if you knew how many people who appear before groups all the time have had to work at it. There is no one single way to deal with shyness, but here are some tips that may help you.

When you're speaking to another person or to a group, remember that your goal is to have them listen to you. To achieve that goal, you must speak in such a way that you can be heard. Try to speak clearly, in a tone that is pleasant, and at a rate that is understandable. Also, try to direct your conversation toward people who have an interest in what you're saying. For example, if you're going to describe a recent vacation to someone who has no interest in your trip, you will soon sense this, and feelings of uneasiness will undoubtedly creep in.

Another important tip for talking to others is to be a good listener. As a good listener, you will be showing others that you are interested in what they are saying. Good listeners find it easier to join into a conversation or to speak before a group because they know what has been said. They have an idea where the conversation is going, and they can more easily join in.

It is unwise to monopolize a conversation. Regardless of how true, how important, or how interesting your words may be, few people like to be in a conversation where they are only listeners. The whole point of a conversation is the exchange of words, thoughts, and ideas. On the other hand, if you seldom or never join in a conversation, people may imagine you are uninterested in what they're saying, and the conversation may simply end.

You mentioned you often say things that you don't mean. This may be the direct result of the shyness you speak of. When you are fearful or worried about your role in a conversation, you may not be thinking about what you are saying. Instead, you are simply concerned about saying something. This results in words without thoughts behind them.

Shyness in conversation is not something anyone can take care of for you. This is a matter that you will have to deal with on your own. Begin by practicing in small groups of people you know. Follow some of the suggestions offered above, and join in conversations whenever possible.

Hey, Mr. McRay,

This is my senior year, and I'm planning to start college after graduation. To help with some of my senior expenses and to put some money away for college, I started working three months ago. I've been working about 12 hours each week in a local restaurant. I work just two evenings and a little on Saturday mornings. The lady I work for said I'm doing real well. A few weeks ago, she asked if I could work a few more hours each week. I told her I would, as long as it didn't get in the way of school.

Last week two of the girls I worked with quit because they couldn't keep up with school and work. Now the manager is pressuring me to work more hours. I don't want to because I barely have enough time now for homework and school activities. I want to explain this to her. Do you think she'll understand? If she doesn't, what would you suggest?

—Signed, Nathan

Job and School Must Be Balanced

Dear Nathan,

The senior year is a transitional period for most high school students. The desire or need to work often conflicts with time demands related to schoolwork and activities. Both educational and social researchers have examined this conflict and as yet have not found a perfect solution. Some high school students flourish when they combine the responsibilities of a job with school and social schedules. Others have some difficulties and serious decisions have to be made.

As you already know, it's unwise to obligate yourself to unreasonable demands on your time. Unless you have discovered a longer day than the rest of us, you only have 24 hours each day. Your concern for school work and activities shows your awareness of this. At the same time, you demonstrate maturity by understanding that when you agree to work for someone, you assume certain responsibilities and make certain commitments. You have already accepted more hours than you initially wanted, so you need feel no guilt if you decide not to accept more. You are more than holding up your end of the original bargain!

You mentioned that you want to talk with your manager. I suggest you do just that as soon as possible. However, before going to her, carefully consider your job in its present context and in the context of the future you are planning for yourself. Ask yourself which will have the greatest positive impact on your life today and in the future—more hours working at the restaurant or more hours devoted to school work and related activities. When you have answered this question for yourself, talk with your manager. I'd certainly hope a manager of a business would understand time limitations. If, however, she doesn't understand your concerns or is not sensitive to them, you have a simple decision to make.

Hey, Mr. McRay,

One of the girls I work with is a real troublemaker. She has been at the restaurant longer than any of us, and she is full time. I just work Thursday evenings and Saturdays. She kind of runs the place, even though she is a waitress like the rest of us. She isn't a head waitress or anything, but she still kind of runs things.

She can be so rude and cutting at times that people are actually afraid of her. Even the manager seems to put up with her attitude. No one wants to speak up to her because of how ugly she can get. If she gets mad at you, she does everything she can to turn other waitresses against you. People act like they like her, and they are nice to her when she's around just so they can stay on her good side. When she's not around, everyone agrees that work goes much easier, and we all get along better. There is always tension when she is around. What is the best way to deal with someone like that?

—Wendy

Co-worker Is a Pain in the Neck

Dear Wendy,

Although the person you describe may be a rather pointed example, most work places have people like this. I'm sure there are some people unlucky enough to have *two* of these "tension-creators" to work with; they have my sympathy!

People act in the ways you describe for many reasons. She may believe that because she's been at the restaurant longer than anyone else, she has a special grant of authority. She may also be an insecure person trying to cover up some personal weaknesses. By intimidating those around her, she can work and associate with them but at the same time keep them at a distance. She may also be the type of person who simply feels the need to assert herself. By giving orders and "controlling" those who she works with, she may be ensuring that few people will attempt to make suggestions, give directions, or point out her errors or shortcomings. She has insulated herself from those around her. Difficult as it is to believe, she may actually be trying to get along. She may feel that those she is working with approve of her actions and attitude. She is unaware of the tension she creates and sees no reasons to change.

Regardless of why, she's still a difficult person to work with, and she has no right to make work so difficult for the rest of you. Someone should explain this situation to her. You, however, are probably not the one to assume this responsibility. As a part-time waitress who only recently began working there, you are in no position to take the lead in this situation. Since the matter you describe involves a number of people at the restaurant, I suggest the manager be made aware of the problem. Though most of you are trying to get along with her, an environment where relationships are based on intimidation will sooner or later blow up. By dealing with the situation now, the manager can avoid a much bigger problem later.

As you prepare to enter the work force, regardless of the field you choose, keep this example in mind. Periodically remind yourself that one person's actions can result in an unpleasant situation for others. Also, strive to develop good relationships with fellow workers. Never depend on fear and intimidation because with them the best you can hope for is a standoff, not a friendship or real cooperation.

Hey, Mr. McRay,

For the summer I'm working at a convenience store. This is the first time I ever worked. My parents won't let me work during school. At first I was real excited about starting to work. I like the money I'm making, but I don't have the free time I used to have. When school was over I just did what I wanted until I went back to school in the fall.

Another problem is that the assistant manager keeps asking me about working weekends during school. I don't want to work during school, and I know my dad won't let me. I'm afraid if I say anything the manager will fire me. I don't want to make him mad because he could cause problems for me when I go to get another job. If you know of anything that you could tell me about this, please answer this letter.

—Yours, Melinda

Take Time to Do the Things You Enjoy

Dear Melinda,

Welcome to the working world! You are making the transition from the carefree years of childhood to the more responsible working years. For most of us, the transition from childhood and youth to the working years begins in the form of a part-time job. This permits us to make the change in more gradual steps than if we had to go from no work to a full-time job or career. The beginning of the working years is a time when you will learn a great deal. The lessons you learn on a part-time job can serve you well throughout your career years, regardless of the career you choose.

You have already begun to learn some of the lessons of the work world. One of the most basic is that working definitely cuts into your free time. Almost everyone who works wishes to have more free time, but few want to see their paycheck reduced. Less free time means you must learn to use it wisely. Be sure to include in it the things you really want to do.

It's important that you fully invest your time and your talents in whatever job you do. There is great satisfaction in doing a job well. For some people, their career brings so much pleasure and fulfillment that they make a total commitment and have little time for anything else. For others, their job provides just a paycheck and no emotional satisfaction. They are willing to make the necessary investment of time and talent, but they don't want the job to dominate their lives. Although it's important to put forth the needed effort and level of commitment to do the job satisfactorily, you needn't allow your job or career to demand all of your time and talents. In fact, allowing a career or job to destroy all aspects of a personal life can quickly result in burnout.

In your current situation, I suggest you commit to do work you are proud of, but tell your manager you don't wish to work during the school year. Plan your free time and make good use of it. Learning to do this now will serve you well when you're in a full-time career.

Hey, Mr. McRay,
        I have started applying for some jobs. I guess the next step will be an interview. I have never been interviewed for a job. Do you have any advice that can help me?

—Yours, Ken

Interview: Looking for a Job That Fits

Dear Ken,

The most basic and very best advice I can offer is "Be yourself!" The purpose of an interview is to see if there is a fit between you and the job you're seeking. If you act, pretend, or lie during an interview, you may get the job, but you and the job may not be right for each other. And being stuck in a job that's not right for you can be worse than no job at all.

Regardless of the type of job you are seeking, it's very important that you arrive for the interview on time. In fact, it's a good idea to arrive a little early. In this way you are showing your potential employer that you are punctual and that you respect your commitments. Remember that first impressions are lasting or, at least, very important. Dressing appropriately for an interview is extremely important and demonstrates respect for your potential employer. If you're seeking employment on a construction crew, it might not be necessary to wear a suit or sport coat. However, if you're applying for a job in a bank or store, a more "dressed-up" appearance is wise. In any case, it is essential that you are clean, neat, and well groomed. It's better to overdress than underdress. Be sure to smile when you meet the interviewer and offer a solid handshake.

Before, during, and after the interview, be courteous and friendly. During the interview, try to be as optimistic as possible. No one enjoys talking to someone with a negative attitude. Don't rush the interview. If you need to, take a few seconds to think before answering the interviewer's questions. On the other hand, don't prolong the interview beyond the time allotted. Be alert to signals that the interviewer has other things to do.

If part of the interview process includes a written application, remember that, as with your appearance, neatness on the application says a great deal about you. And be as honest as possible! For example, if you indicate that you can operate a computer and you can't, you may later face some real embarrassment, and you may even lose your job.

Before completing an application or going for an interview, take a good look at yourself. You may have more to offer an employer than you think. It's unwise to suggest to an employer you can do things that you can't, but it's just as unwise to fail to mention your strengths, talents, and abilities. For example, if you don't have specific job experience, but you managed a Little League team, mention that.

Earlier I suggested that a job interview is an opportunity for an employer to see if you are the right person for the job and if the job is right for you. Don't hesitate to ask some questions. In fact, failure to ask some job-related questions may send the message that you are not interested. When you leave, offer another handshake and thank the person for the opportunity to be interviewed.

Finally, don't be upset or discouraged if you don't get the job. There are many reasons why you may be turned down. Some of these may deal with you directly, and others may have nothing to do with you. For example, the person(s) interviewing you may have determined that they want someone older or younger than you. Even though they are interviewing "all" applicants, you can do nothing to meet the hidden criteria the employer has established. No matter what happens, use the experience to your benefit the next time you interview for a job.

Finding job opportunities, applying for them, and being interviewed are very important and exciting challenges. Good luck!

About the Author

Dr. Michael R. McGough, originally from Johnstown, Pennsylvania, received his undergraduate education at the University of Pittsburgh, graduating with a degree in secondary education in 1972. He earned a Master's degree in 1977 from Western Maryland College and received his public school administrative certification from Shippensburg University in 1988. In 1989, he graduated with honors from Pennsylvania State University with a doctorate in adult education.

Dr. McGough's career in public education includes fifteen years as a social studies teacher and twelve years as a school administrator. He is currently a central office administrator. Dr. McGough has served as an adjunct professor of education and political science at four different colleges. Since 1976, he has been a Licensed Battlefield Guide with the National Park Service in Gettysburg. Dr. McGough has written several other books and numerous articles on a variety of topics. In addition to *Hey, Mr. McRay...*, he is the author of three other long-running newspaper columns: "Through Uncle Sam's Window," an American history column; "Something to Think About," a general interest column focusing on the lessons of daily life; and "If I Were You," a personal advice column.

Dr. McGough is married, the father of two grown children, and currently resides in Adams County, Pennsylvania.